Moral Memoranda From John Howard Yoder:

Conversations on Law, Ethics and the Church between a Mennonite Theologian and a Hoosier Lawyer

by Thomas L. Shaffer
Robert and Marion Short Professor of Law Emeritus
University of Notre Dame

Wipf and Stock Publishers
199 West 8th Avenue, Eugene OR 97401

Moral Memoranda From John Howard Yoder
By Thomas L. Shaffer
Copyright 2002 by Thomas L. Shaffer

ISBN:1-59244-037-1

Wipf and Stock Publishers
199 West 8th Avenue
Eugene, OR 97401

TABLE OF CONTENTS

Preface		iii
Chapter One	Christians in Pluralist America	1
A.	Religious Argument in Public	2
B.	Religious Argument in Church	16
Chapter Two	War, Peace, Lethal State Power, and Legal Ethics	27
A.	Ethical Groundwork	28
B.	Just War	32
C.	Capital Punishment	42
D.	Civil Disobedience	46
Chapter Three	Ethics and Eschatology	51
A.	Eschatology	51
B.	Natural Law Jurisprudence	55
C.	On Using Stories in Christian Ethics	62
D.	Feminist Jurisprudence	74
Chapter Four	On the Possibility of a Christian Law School	76
A.	The Law School in Church	77
B.	Legal Order	86
C.	Pedagogy	93
Chapter Five	Legal Issues	101
Epilogue	On Learning About Law from John Howard Yoder	115

Preface: The Last We Heard...*

John Howard Yoder, prophet and theologian, died in his office at Notre Dame on December 30, 1997, the day after his seventieth birthday. Peter Steinfels's obituary in the New York Times of January 7, 1998, described my friend and colleague Yoder as "a Mennonite theologian whose writings on Christianity and politics had a major impact on contemporary Christian thinking about the church and social ethics." Mr. Steinfels did not describe Yoder's thought as jurisprudence; neither, for that matter, did Yoder. But there was (and is), throughout Yoder's scholarship, an implicit theology of law, a jurisprudence and a legal ethic. Much of what John wrote about law was written to me, as he helped me with ideas I was developing in my own published work, or about me, as he commented on my work. This book is mostly about what John wrote to me, although I have, through the kindness of Anne-Marie Yoder, been able to locate and use his thoughts on the law as he directed them to others.

John was, Mr. Steinfels wrote, first and foremost a pacifist. Mr. Steinfels quoted John's sometime colleague at Notre Dame, the Methodist theologian Stanley Hauerwas: "After World War II and the criticism of pacifism by Reinhold Niebuhr, Christian nonviolence had lost credibility. Yoder turned that around." Pacifism is, of course, a problem for lawyers, and law and lawyers a problem for pacifists. It has become a commonplace among law teachers in the modern United States that the law rests on lethal force; how a pacifist practices law in the shadow of that lethal force is a significant moral and theological agenda: There are lawyers who do it, of course, not least some, including myself, who gain perspective if not comfort from Yoder's eclectic way of fashioning a theological ethic. John and I exchanged views on law and pacifism from time to time. The subtle thrust of that development–noticeable in these pages, perhaps--was that I was myself becoming a pacifist, mostly because I was reading and thinking about John's astounding

---

*The preface is reworked from a part of the editor's article "The Jurisprudence of John Howard Yoder," 22 Legal Studies Forum 473 (1998), and is used here, and later in this book, with permission.

iii

Preface

moral theology.

Community

Beyond that, or within it, Mr. Steinfels wrote, John was (as Hauerwas is) a theologian who taught that "the work of Jesus was not a new set of ideals or principles for reforming or even revolutionizing society, but the establishment of a new community, a people that embodied forgiveness, sharing, and self-sacrificing love in its rituals and discipline. In that sense, the visible church for him was not the bearer of Christ's message; it was itself to be the message.

"Mr. Yoder understood the church as a creative minority that would always live in a way that contrasted with the surrounding society. He criticized all tendencies for the church to assume a blanket responsibility for the ethics of the secular world." Much of what John wrote to me, a lawyer anxious to be a Christian, and the collected sermons, lectures, and essays in John's late book, For the Nations (1997), and in the posthumously published To Hear the Word (2001), demonstrate (continuing to quote from the obituary by Peter Steinfels) that John "rejected [the] charge that he was calling for the church to withdraw into isolation, and he devoted much of his writing to demonstrating how neither his pacifism nor his sectarianism prevented the church from providing a crucial witness to the secular world or from combating a host of injustices."

Mr. Steinfels took into account John's older and widely read book, The Politics of Jesus (1972; 2nd ed. 1994), and, even more, a lifetime of Christian witness that began among the Mennonites in France, when John was eighteen. "As a writer, Mr. Yoder was clear and direct, never skirting differences but always trying to represent his opponents fairly. A proponent of nonviolence, he nonetheless criticized many of the varieties of pacifism advocated by Christians as sentimental, resting on naively optimistic, utopian views of human nature or on strictly utilitarian calculations of pacifism's effectiveness compared with other forms of opposing evil."

In addition to, or threaded through, John's project in Christian social ethics is a theology of law. Those threads became more visible for me, over more than a decade, when John turned, always with generosity, from his own work–to mine, to what a Hoosier lawyer, teaching across campus, was trying to learn about Christian ethics.

On Being a Christian and a Lawyer

Mennonites, only a few of them lawyers, tend to shy away from legal solutions, and therefore from discussion of legal solutions. I have often quoted

Preface

something John said to a Notre Dame college student of his, who later became a law student of mine. This young man, impressed by John's teaching, asked John, his theology teacher, if a Christian could be a lawyer--and then proceeded to say why he thought not. John heard him out before he said, "Well, maybe a Christian cannot be a lawyer."

But the young man came to law school anyway. And John later told me he would not have pressed his answer to our student's question. The better question, John later said to me, is whether the things a lawyer does in modern America are the things a person who proposed to follow Jesus might do. That is, I finally decided, after many uses of the earlier quotation, and after many letters and memos from John, the way to see the issue. And that is the way our student took what he learned from John; he has, I think, lived with John's later question in mind for three decades as a lawyer in America. He has learned that there are many things a Christian working in the law can do, and, no doubt, some things she must not do.

One can think of this later way of putting the question–I do think of it–as provoking an array of responses on a spectrum: At one end of the spectrum are those in teaching, in the church, on law faculties, and in the press, who insist that the question--a moral question--has to be answered from a position within the modern American nation-state. The most prominent lawyer (law-teacher) voices from this end of the spectrum say it is immoral for a believer who is a lawyer to give religious reasons for her jurisprudence, or for a believer who holds legal power to follow her faith in deciding whether and how to invoke or impose coercive state power. A modification, only slightly to the left, would permit a believer to consult her faith when she exercises state power, or would recognize that she is bound to do so if she really is a believer, but then holds that it is immoral for her to be candid about what she has done. She should keep her religious reasons to herself.

At the other end of the spectrum are those in communities of faith who decline participation in the law--as voters, or as lawyers, or as holders of governmental office. Ernst Troeltsch called these believers "sectarian," a term Mr. Steinfels picked up, and one that becomes pejorative among those who accuse withdrawn believers of being irresponsible. John also took issue with those at this left end of the spectrum; his reasoning with them–like his wary treatment of Troeltsch's word–makes up much of the contents of For the Nations and To Hear the Word, and came up often in his messages to me, many of which are gathered in Chapter One of this book.

In between are a number of nuanced theological positions, and what I think of as a struggle among theologians who "do" social ethics, (and among lawyers who try to locate Jewish and Christian legal ethics), to locate an argument that accepts, as Martin Luther did, that the Kingdom of Faith has and should have influence--open influence--on the Kingdom of the Law (whether or not the bridge

Preface

has lanes in both directions, that is, whether or not Luther's Kingdom of the Law should have influence on the Kingdom of Faith).

Speaking to the religious ("sectarian") end of the spectrum, John argued for a religious jurisprudence that speaks out, whether or not those at the other end of the spectrum think it should: **"[T]he love of a sovereign God drives us into concern for the social order.... God does not simply tell us to accept the existing order; he tells us also that it must change,"** John wrote in For the Nations. John turned to the Bible as if it were a charter for law and government and--just in case O.W. Holmes, Jr., might have been listening--the source as well of a theory of history. And not only a theory of history, but a position that itself is history. John cited as political–and, I think, as jurisprudential–examples William Penn, William Lloyd Garrison, and such 19th century American evangelical leaders as Alexander Campbell, all of whom were "sectarians" demonstrating **"concern for healthy political life.... This long history refutes the notion that the type of community stance which the sociologist calls 'sectarian' is without wider interest or impact,"** John said.

Still toward the left end of the spectrum, John addressed the moral issues in civil disobedience, in For the Nations, in writing to me, and in an essay, reproduced here (Chapter Two), that he submitted reluctantly to one of Notre Dame's legal journals. He was wary of those (believers) who practice non-violent political and legal pressure in order to take power in the name of justice; he said of that position that it is **"less than loving and no less intrinsically sinful than another kind of warfare."** Here especially he would not admit that his demanding biblical jurisprudence was weakened when it appeared to be ineffective: Claiming at least passing support from H. Richard Niebuhr, he wrote in For the Nations. **"[I]t may be all right sometimes to acknowledge that there is nothing we can do to fix the world.... If we saw our obedience more as praising God and less as running his world for him, we would be less prey to both despair and disobedience."**

John's biblical touchstone, offered from within his Anabaptist tradition, offered publicly, and offered as a helping hand to me, was what the Prophet Jeremiah wrote to the captive Israelites in Babylon: "Seek the welfare of any city to which I have carried you off, and pray to the Lord for it; on its welfare your welfare will depend" (Jeremiah 29:7, N.E.B.). **"For Jeremiah it is mission,"** John argued; it was not merely a way to get along until the captivity ended, but a long-term project Jews undertook before the Temple in Jerusalem was rebuilt.

Advice to the Mainline Church

Toward the middle of the spectrum, John offered persistent witness to what I think of as the mainline church, the large, established Protestant

Preface

denominations and the American Roman Catholic Church. John spoke to these mainline Christians from the untapped resources of their own tradition, rather than as an Anabaptist. Here, like the late radical Christian lawyer William Stringfellow, an Episcopalian,** John invoked references from the Apostle Paul about the powers and dominions of the world, **"[t]he Pauline vision according to which 'the powers' which frame our lives are at one and the same time both creatures of God for our good and oppressors," as he put it in For the Nations.** The powers in modern American life are represented in what John might there have identified (but did not) as American civil religion--in the American dream, which is made up of strands, like a rope: **"the aggressive hope for history of Puritan Protestantism, the philosophical credibility of progress as a cosmic drive, and the experience of white America's successful seizure of the continent."**

The question for Christians--the question John put when he got American civil religion in his sights--is whether it is possible to keep on believing when one of these strands breaks, when civil religion appears less and less Christian and more and more idolatrous. (Civil religion is, for one thing, not likely to see suffering–suffering servant Israel, the cross–as a means of social change.) Those in the alternative church (John often called it the believers church), by contrast, leave deadlines and mechanisms up to God; they see no correlation between the ultimate victory of God and present prosperity or power. John's argument in the mainline church was that this byproduct of faithfulness belongs as much to Methodists and Presbyterians as it belongs to Mennonites.

More distinctively, and more legally, those in the alternative church do not seek political solutions through violence: **"That violence in the cause of freedom is morally in a different category from violence for other causes is an ancient notion, usually (in our history) correlated with white triumphalism."** As this, from For the Nations, suggests, John thought of Dr. King's community: **"An oppressed community is sustained by a hope which is not verified first of all by experience, and therefore cannot be falsified by apparent defeat. The community which sustained the hope was first of all authorized to hope not by its experience of**

**The late William Stringfellow, who died in 1985, was a radical lawyer and a radical Christian. He was also a prolific publisher. Two late sources are a post-mortem collection of his writings, A Keeper of the Word: Selected Writings of William Stringfellow (1994), edited by Bill Wylie-Kellermann; and a collection of commentaries about him, Radical Christian and Exemplary Lawyer (1995), edited by Andrew W. McThenia, Jr. Stringfellow's books are listed at page 181 of the latter volume.

Preface

effective militancy but by singing and preaching and mothering and eating together in the light of the good news.... [T]here are other patterns of power for change than the victory of the good guys. That the Crucified One is now 'seated at the right hand of the Father' means that 'he has the <u>whole</u> world in his hands,' without its being in <u>our</u> hands."****

Most of what follows is from letters, memos, and notes John wrote me during the two decades he helped me with my attempt to work out a Christian theology for lawyers. I attempt, after this preface, to keep my own theorizing off stage (I often bite my tongue in doing it), so that it is Yoder who speaks. In a few cases I have come across letters or memos John wrote to others that have not been published. These were either communications he sent me a copy of, or

---

***One of John's principal publishers, Eerdmans, in its Spring-Summer 1998 catalogue, published a short obituary which contains this supplementary information:

"A Mennonite theologian most widely known for his work in Christian social ethics, Yoder was born in Smithville, Ohio, in 1927. He earned bachelor's and master's degrees from Goshen College, then studied with Karl Barth as a doctoral student at the University of Basel, Switzerland. After serving as a Mennonite Central Committee relief worker in Europe, Yoder returned home to teach at Goshen College. From 1965 to 1984 he taught at Goshen Biblical Seminary, which later became the Associated Mennonite Biblical Seminary, and he served as president of the institution from 1970 to 1973. He spent the last quarter century of his career as professor of theology at the University of Notre Dame.

"Probably Yoder's greatest influence has come through his book <u>The Politics of Jesus</u>, first published in 1972 and now in its second edition. About this enduring work, Stanley Hauerwas has written in <u>The Christian Century</u>, "I am convinced that when Christians look back on this century of theology in America, <u>The Politics of Jesus</u> will be seen as a new beginning." Other important volumes by Yoder include <u>Christian Attitudes to War, Peace, and Revolution</u> and <u>The Priestly Kingdom</u>.

"Yoder's rich body of work spans the fields of systematic theology, Christian ethics, war and peace studies, sixteenth-century Protestant history, missiology, and ecumenism. Yet, in the face of such accomplishments, Yoder steadfastly maintained a bearing of Christian humility, insisting instead on turning admiration toward Jesus Christ–the sole focus of his life's work. Peter Steinfels aptly summarized this abiding characteristic of Yoder's life when he reflected in the <u>New York Times</u> that Yoder 'kept his achievements subordinated to his faith.' Both his work and his example of faith will be missed."

Preface

communications I found copies of in his files. In a few cases I use published excerpts, some from Notre Dame publications, some from reviews I wrote of his books.

The material from John Howard Yoder, all from my files or from files of his that were kindly loaned to me by his family, is used with the permission of his wife, Anne-Marie Yoder. It is, of course, informal, a fact that compels me to include here a note he wrote me, when I asked his permission to quote from one of his memos in footnotes to a published essay of mine:

"None of the things you propose to quote from me as part of your <u>basso continuo</u> would embarrass me or deceive the reader, so I have no reason to withhold permission to quote. It probably would be good however to indicate somehow the very informal status of these passages; that they are from ad hoc comments on the margins...rather than a coherent paper of mine which your readers might look up.... [There are] more and less careful kinds of memoranda." (Jan. 20, 1994)

Tom Shaffer
Notre Dame, Indiana
September 2002

* A note for the reader: In order to reflect the conversational reality of this text, John Howard Yoder's words are bold type and Thomas Shaffer's are in plain type.

x

Chapter One

Christians in Pluralist America

John Yoder believed in argument, in public, in support of the legal and political dispositions his faith led him to have. He did not believe in withdrawal from the public square. John, having decided to argue, thought that argument should be as effective as possible–so that he was usually willing to argue in the language of those he addressed and in the terms set by those he opposed. But he had no problem, as many academics do–many of them lawyers, some of them theologians–with making religious arguments in public. I think in fact he tended to favor being candid about the scriptural and theological basis for his arguments, because candid religious argument on a political or legal issue (care for the poor, for example, or capital punishment) might influence his hearers and even his opponents toward belief–might influence them, that is, in a personal, religious way.

Those who argue for religious argument in public, against the moral argument that we are not being fair to unbelievers, tend (as I do) to play down the dangers of coercion that lurk in our national and legal past. John understood, better than anybody I know, where the history of coercion in public argument came from–an origin that has more to do with religious coercion than with modern, liberal opposition to religion, and an origin that, John feared, was not as ancient as defenders of religious argument (myself included) might think.

In any event, the modern American issue of religious argument in public has been prominent in recent decades among politicians, theologians, and lawyers, with an array of positions stretching from those who say religious argument on a public question is immoral to those who make distinctions among legal and political issues (allowing religious argument on some of them but not others) to those (some evangelical Christians, Roman Catholic Bishops on some issues) who focus on religious arguments to the exclusion of other political arguments.

A. RELIGIOUS ARGUMENT IN PUBLIC

Here is a brief introduction to John's thought on the point, borrowed from my published essay in the Legal Studies Forum and some quoted from To Hear the Word (excerpts from each, here and below, are used with permission):

To those who argue that it is immoral for people of faith to invoke their faith as bearing on public issues in a secular legal order,[1] John's response was complex. He was willing to discuss political (and legal) issues in the "language" of his critics; he was willing, I suppose, not to use biblical language where biblical language did not communicate; and he was willing to accept small victories when his jurisprudence told him to try for more. The authority that faith gives, he wrote, "is not coercion but trust, which is 'the law within law.'" Fidelity and relevance are not a "null-sum trade-off." And therefore, as Martin Luther might have put it, the person of faith can use the language of the dominions and powers and take the risk that he might be right.

Still, Yoder was not willing to hide his faith and his witness, not willing to hide either what it bade him say nor the deepest reasons for his saying it, not willing that Christianity be only **"the general label for anyone's good intentions,"** as he put it. **"Not whether the message is for all humankind is the question, but what the message is."**

Which, of course, sounds contradictory if not paradoxical: How could he argue in public, using the language of American civil religion, and not thereby violate his determination to be witness to the fact that the Kingdom has come, that Jesus is Lord? Yoder's answer was to accept small victories, incremental gain, and circumstantial agreement–precisely because he did not see himself and the believers church of which he was both member and spokesman as responsible for making the

---

[1] The position of those who oppose religious argument in public is a moral argument. It says it is immoral for a believer to argue from creed, theology, or scripture, when the issue is political or legal and when those listening and on the other side include non-believers. Michael J. Perry, a Roman Catholic and a law teacher (Wake Forest), is prolific in defending religious arguments in these contexts. His essay "Why Political Reliance on Religiously Grounded Morality Is Not Illegitimate in a Liberal Democracy," 36 Wake Forest Law Review 217 (2001), covers his current thinking on the matter and shows him to be in dialogue about it with law teachers such as Mark Tushnet and Kent Greenawalt, and political philosophers such as Richard Rorty and John Rawls.

legal order work. It is a matter of seeking the welfare of the city, not seeking to take control of the city. Jesus is already in control.

Beyond that, he wrote in To Hear the Word, it is a matter of reaching out: **"To confess Christ as Lord differs from some other fundamental stances, in fact, in that its very structure does claim to incorporate other value data. It does this neither by affirming them all (which would be a mindless pluralism) nor by specifically denying any of them, but by a nuanced interlocking which understands other values as at once created, fallen, in the process of being judged, and in the process of being led toward restoration.... The most adequate modern effort to render this complex vision uses the Pauline system of 'principalities and powers.'"** (Pp. 58-59)

Yoder on Steven Carter

John and I corresponded about the reduction of religion in America to what Steven Carter, a Christian lawyer, had, in his popular book The Culture of Disbelief,[2] called a hobby. John was helping me with a review essay on Carter's influential book. Some of the issue had to do with civil libertarian lawyers litigating over such things as Christmas decorations in public schools. Some of it had to do with lawyers, judges, and politicians making religious arguments in public forums.

I agree that the polarized defensiveness with which A.C.L.U. types and atheists overdo the wall of separation is wrong. But I would try to be more of an historian, asking where the defensiveness came from that is [now] being overdone.... [I]t is very misleading to begin the story of the problems of toleration in the middle. It is not that anybody important wanted to keep elite neocons like [Richard] Neuhaus from living their faith in the public square. It is that old-fashioned conservatives thought that the only way for them to act in the public square was to exclude the Jews and the Quakers.

---

[2]Full title, The Culture of Disbelief: How American Law and Politics Trivialize Religious Devotion (1993). I reviewed the book at 62 University of Cincinnati Law Review 1601 (1994). I had some trouble, as, I think, John would have, with Carter's tolerance of Constantinian theology; I rejoiced at Carter's principal defense of religious argument, though–at his insistence that Christian faith is more than a hobby. The last bit of the review: "There are two agendas here, not one. The first and safer agenda...would return America to the grand claim made by our forefathers–few were foremothers–that America is 'God's New Israel,' a city on a hill, the righteous empire. The other agenda is religious. It invokes the manifest history of Israel, the Suffering Servant of God, and of the Cross, as symbols of what people do to one another in the name of the law."

Moral Memoranda From John Howard Yoder

Don't complain about overdoing the secularization without recognizing that it was the natural response (overdone, as anything is when made legal) of victims to the dominion of the Erastians. The need to keep the Bible out of the schools is the extrapolated exaggeration of the victory of the Tolstoyan Darrow against [the] Tolstoyan Bryan. The reason we got into the box where assertions based on faith are especially constricted is the long history of the people who made assertions based on faith coercively. Failure to "make space for all available options" was invented not by the A.C.L.U. but by the Erastians.

Part of the problematic [Carter gets into] if [he is] not satisfied with "hobby" status is that somebody has to get into the business of accrediting which are the entities that qualify for the status of non-hobby religions with rights to a place on the podium. If native Americans smoking peyote, how about the Klan burning crosses? Scientology? A mail-order degree mill issuing certificates of ordination?

Carter "relentlessly discounts" the danger than anyone would impose an orthodoxy. I may share his trust that good law-school liberals will never fall back into obscurantism, but I still don't trust his lack of attentiveness to the intrinsic danger of letting power bearers use God language.

God's New Israel with a mission to subjugate the world [which is how I had described American civil religion] is one religion; the Suffering Servant is another. The choice is not between putting religion first and putting the state first. (It would be that for the A.C.L.U.) It is between an imperial and genocidal religion and a Suffering Servant one. (Dec. 9, 1993)

Yoder on Mary Ann Glendon

I tend to feel that Mary Ann Glendon's description of what has been wrong with the piecemeal approach to "two clauses" [in the first amendment to the federal constitution] and the notion of "separation" as such make sense. I support her dissatisfaction with reducing all other rights to "speech" and making only individuals rights-bearers. Reading her makes me all the more convinced of the pertinence of the criticisms which I have been making...about the historilessness with which you lawyers read texts.

She does recognize, as some do not, that the purpose of the first amendment in the <u>federal</u> constitution was to leave the states free in that realm, including keeping establishment. What she does not recognize is the vibrant and fluid situation for which that compromise was an ultimately unstable solution.

The first mistake which seems to be frequent in this field is failure to recognize the weight of the precedents of Roger Williams and William Penn, whereby the anti-establishment alternative was made viable. There is usually some reference to the Virginia Baptists, because they got into the paper trail via

Jefferson, but it is usually ignored that the argument is much older.

Another mistake is the failure to recognize the significance of the very term "Bill of Rights" as a pointer back to a British predecessor exactly one century older. The reason that that matters is that it should point back to the still older polemic of British Puritans from Browne to Milton. For these people the reason for freedom of assembly, press, and speech was neither individualistic nor associationist but theocratic. Because the Word of God demands to be publicly proclaimed, neither Elizabeth nor any of her successors has any right to control it. That is why Williams and then Penn demonstrated long before the Virginia Baptists that it is perfectly possible to administer a Christian commonwealth in line with one's convictions about the Word of God, yet without the ruler's regulating assembly, press, or speech. Williams and Penn were in no sense secularist or pluralist or individualist. They were Christian theocrats, but the order they believed God wants in the civil realm does not govern belief or assembly....

I have not read of anyone in your guild inclined to study [the] earlier British experience of the [effect] of the Radical Reformation on government.... [T]he official Reformation...made little contribution to the Bills of Rights. It was in fact the power which the Bills of Rights were set up to restrain. (April 20, 1993)

Ways to Influence the Public Debate

In my review of Carter's book, I had contrasted the "gathered" church and the church of Christendom with what I called the "witnessing" church that does not disdain influence: "It claims influence; it even fashions its arguments...so that they will be heard and understood by nonbelievers as well as believers." I thought I was writing as Yoder's pupil.

Your avowal of "trying to influence," which is the basically right evangelical stance, might be protected against misinterpretation by explaining that there are also some good evangelical grounds for avoiding some kinds of "trying to influence," such as establishment, coercion, defamation. Not all avoidance of "trying to influence" is weak-willed positionlessness. I still prefer the A.C.L.U. to the creationists....I don't think there is any tension between large vision and particularity; only Hebraic monotheism sees the world whole. (Dec. 29, 1992)

In To Hear the Word, John wrote: "A pietist or a prescientific social thinker might say more simply that defending my rights means not trusting God. A more sophisticated analyst would add that it means not trusting other people, not trusting dialogue and forgiveness, not trusting conflict resolution and due process; it claims instead that one has no choice but to manipulate, to use nondialogical power, and to accumulate and preserve one's own economic advantage at the cost of wider sharing. 'Taking thought for the morrow' is what some call 'an ethic of responsibility.' We must control events because God won't. Its basic moral mood is utilitarian. It puts security above solidarity. It privileges one's own party in calculating the common good.

"From all of this we have backed into a functional definition of what 'trusting God' would mean in concrete social terms. It would mean that our calculations of the common good would not begin by privileging our own perspective, and would not be used to assign to ourselves or to our party the authority to impose our vision or our rights on others by authority or by applying greater power. To trust God is then to trust in dialogue and due process, repentance and the common search. Does this have something to say about economic justice and 'national security'?

"There is a deep commonality between the daring to share that is enjoined for the disciples' economic life...and the love for enemy that is commended in the realm of conflict.... Both risk themselves at the hand of open process over which one is ready to relinquish control.

"Proclamation and prayer derived from the coming of the Kingdom give reason to trust that such renunciation is not going to be generally suicidal, though it may be situationally costly. Heralding the kingdom (Matt. 3:2; 4:17; 10:7) and the commitment in prayer to its coming (6:10) do not replace sober planning with blind faith, nor social analysis with unthinking obedience. They change the calculation of common good. They place realism in a framework of faith and hope." (p. 37)

Yoder on Erastus (and Robert E. Rodes, Jr.)

John often referred to a theological position on the church within the state as "Erastian." And often John and I both, when using that word, were thinking of the description of it in the work of our colleague Robert E. Rodes, Jr., who wrote, "I define Erastianism as a tendency to see the institutional church as only one of a variety of institutions through which a Christian society conforms itself to the will of God.... It seems...to be in keeping with what Erastus (1524-1583), a Swiss amateur theologian writing in Heidelberg had in mind." (Lay Authority and Reformation in the English Church 1 [1982]). Each of the three of us, in using the term, then, raised what I think of as the "religion and law" question, as distinguished from the "church-state" question that tends to describe the efforts of lawyers, judges, and politicians when they analyze the "wall of separation" supposedly erected by American constitutional law. John, more than anyone else, taught me to think of an alternative scholarly field, "religion and law," that involves not what American democracy is to do about the church, but what the church is to do about American democracy. He rarely agreed, though, with my way of stating the issue.

When thinking about whether the Christian community should have

ambitious visions for the wider world, including the civil order with its basis in coercion, it is possible to use "Erastian" in the way you do. I would however point out that church historians use the word more often when dealing with a different agenda, namely how the institutional church should be governed. Johannes Oecolampadius and Martin Buber and John Calvin believed that the church as institution, i.e., the agency which determines who has the right to preach and to administer the sacraments in the parish building, should have its own agency of government constituted of a body of elders.

They believed that it was appropriate that the elders might be named in a process which the civil order would monitor and that [those chosen] then would be good citizens and loyal subjects, but they insisted that it should be internally self-governing. John Calvin in fact left Geneva because the city council would not give him this amount of relative autonomy, and only went back to Geneva when they were willing to invite him on his own terms. On the other hand, Huldrych Zwingli, his disciple Bullinger and his disciple Erastus believed that the government of the functions which I referred to above should be no less the business of the civil rulers than should be all the other functions of the state. The church was in that respect no different from the post office or the soup kitchen for the poor or the militia.

Thus the issue of governance is the one for which in church history we use the name of Erastus. While that position goes back to Zwingli and Bullinger, it was from the writings of Erastus that is was more widely propagated in the world in which the Anglican establishment was settling in the latter half of the century. (Jan. 20, 1993)

Yoder on Hugo Grotius (and Robert E. Rodes, Jr.)

I had, in a manuscript I sent to John, mentioned Bob Rodes's paper on modern American Catholic universities (published in an anthology edited by Father Theodore M. Hesburgh, C.S.C., president emeritus of the University of Notre Dame).[3] The main argument Rodes had–one I thought John would have found cordial–was that the intellectual common ground American Catholic universities have had with secular higher education in the country has disappeared or become trivial. Bob's argument was for a new agenda, one that would advertently refer to the Second Vatican Council's document Gaudium et Spes, and more generally to modern Catholic social teaching:

---

[3]Robert E. Rodes, Jr., "Catholic Universities and the New Pluralism," in Theodore M. Hesburgh (ed.), The Challenge and Promise of a Catholic University (1994), at 305.

Catholics today are challenged not merely on discrete points of doctrine or practice, but on what is most fundamental to a Christian vision of human beings and their affairs....

(Secular) institutions have portions of a proud tradition still in place, and great ideas and noble causes continue to find shelter on their campuses. We can admire them, support them, and learn from them. But we cannot allow them to set our agenda for us....

We have...both a new problem and a new opportunity. A new problem because we no longer have an extensive and well defined set of concerns of which we can safely follow the mainstream. A new opportunity because if we are faithful to our calling, we will not have to follow the mainstream. We can lead.

But the earlier parts of Bob's paper described the disappearing common ground as one that rested on the teaching of Hugo Grotius (d. 1645). John took exception to Bob's saying that Grotius provided Western Christianity "the basis for an orderly pluralist society and a coherent pluralist intellectual life." John responded to the historical argument in a memo to Bob, copy to me:

Whether it was worth arguing the point I raised depends on how much argumentative weight can fittingly be carried by a metaphor. Watching the identity argument around "Catholic" Notre Dame, and around "the University," has brought me to suspect that issues are not best served by the profusion of images and metaphors which are drawn into the discussion. My way of implementing that doubt about the utility of a metaphor is usually to take it seriously rather than to ignore it.

Grotius has become for historians, in your field and even in mine, the symbol of the "New World Order" initiated by the Peace of Westphalia, even though he was dead before the treaty was signed.

What that "new order" meant politically was an agreed standoff among the crowns of Europe. They did not agree to religious liberty for their subjects, or to mutual respect between faiths, but to reciprocal recognition of each others' sovereignty, to doing diplomacy and fighting war by the rules, and to not fighting about confessions. That being established, then it made sense for Grotius to codify the great classical heritage of the rules for fighting fair.

Calvinists, Lutherans, and Catholics who found themselves in the territory of sovereigns of another "confession" were to be tolerated, but there was no freedom of immigration or evangelization. A ruler was free to tolerate Jews or Mennonites if he felt tolerant, but he did not have to. Nothing kept the King of France from revoking in 1685 the toleration of Calvinists which had already (previously to Westphalia) been assured by the Edict of Nantes. Thus there is a considerable metaphorical stretch between

(a) a tactic of reciprocal tolerance between heads of state, dividing

categories of issues between those the parties agree on, which suffice for regulating inter-crown relations, and those they differ on, which do not matter for diplomacy and fighting fair, and

(b) applying an analogous separation of issues to denominational communities in America, none of them defined territorially, most of them not monarchical, none of them sovereign, none of them able even in concept either to win or to lose a war.

Any metaphor is possible moving from one realm to another. I do not challenge that there is some commonality between the realms, in that issues are divided by category, some of them not worth fighting for, and others subjected by agreement of all parties to fighting by the rules. But I doubt that that very abstract commonality will stretch to be really illuminating to describe the differences that separate Bloomington, Northwestern, and Notre Dame.

My impression is that that consideration, about the limits of metaphor, might if taken seriously render moot my other objection to what Tom was playing back, namely your description of what Grotius did..., "seek out and articulate common ground." For a diplomat trying to structure the pacification of South Africa or the provinces left over from the U.S.S.R. or Yugoslavia, or Carter or Kissinger shuttling between Cairo and Jerusalem, or a local pol trying to build a health care program in Washington or public school policy in Chicago, "seeking for common ground" would be an empirically-based process, picking the minds of the parties, determining what they could all live with. That is what I think Tom's allusion would suggest to his readers. That is not what Grotius did.

For Grotius that classical commonality was in fact there, like bedrock not far below the surface of the land. It took no searching and no consensus-building, only a little déblayage, sweeping-away of surface dust. The "already there" was the commonality which Calvinist, Lutheran, and Catholic power-bearers, both political sovereigns and scholars, all assumed to be valid since it did not question but rather supported their fusion of monarchy with the established church and university. It said nothing about the option for the poor or even about democratic due process. It could tolerate a degree of pre-democratic consultation within government in the Calvinist nations, but that was not what Grotius codified, since it was the rules of due process among governments which he organized. That "already there" substance was the fusion of classical antiquity and Judeo-Christian monotheism which had taken over that part of Europe between the time of Constantine and that of Charlemagne, and which no head of state in 1648 thought of challenging.

What Grotius (or rather the age of Westphalia for which he is the symbol—we have not tested to what extent he was its creator) stands for is adjusting the Constantinian establishment to the breakup of the nations and the state-church confessions, while still saving Establishment. That settlement saved the principles of established religion and monarchy within each state, by determining that what the three state-church confessions differed about was not, and did not need to be, subject to adjudication by diplomacy and war.

That was a good arrangement. If nations had lived up to Grotius' vision for war according to the rules, history for the last three centuries would have been very different. But of course they did not; so it should be considered a provocative utopian vision, not a real strategy nor an accurate description of anything that worked.

Even at its best, the Westphalian compromise was not good news for Jews and the Anabaptists, nor for the poor or the "colonial peoples." Nor did it cast any light on the quite different clashes going on at the same time in England, which were to issue ultimately in a different kind of conflict resolution: more viable, not between heads of state but rather among elites and minorities within a single commonwealth. The English solution was better for Baptists and Quakers and Roman Catholics, and ultimately for Jews.

Maybe I should argue that the arrangement of the Bills of Rights, the basic [English] one of 1689 and the derivative [American] one of 1789, would be a better metaphor for the cohabitation of diverse religious communities in the American intellectual world than that of Grotius, since the metaphor would not have to stretch so far. For now, though, I would rather not argue that, since my prior impression is that the use of any master metaphor, even a better one, creates new confusion before it illuminates.

If we were going to use the models from the continental 17th [century] to illuminate the problem of pluralism in the American university, the <u>tertium comparationis</u> would not be how the separate rulers agreed not to fight about some things and to fight fair about some others. It would rather be the internal monarchy which remains. That is what Harvard and Brown, Notre Dame and Northwestern all had in 1900. State and federal governments chartered them and left them alone, so that each could remain a clerical minichristendom where the denominational authorities ran the school. It is that clerical control whose waning permits the charges of betrayal that [James T.] Burtchaell and [George M.] Marsden chronicle and bewail. This does not mean that Burtchaell and Marsden want clerical control; but the qualities whose loss they notice were dependent on that when they did obtain. This shows the importance of distinguishing between causative explanations and illuminating metaphors.

"The new pluralism" is thus not the product of a loss of the Grotian vision. Its components came from outside the world the metaphor describes. Yet it may have been fostered by weaknesses in the intellectual underpinnings of the Grotian vision, <u>i.e.</u>, in the notion that there is in fact "back there" a common Greco-Roman-Jewish bedrock which all power-bearers will agree is classical. Grotius could do that about the rules for monarchs' fighting fair. He did not do it, and Hesburgh could not do it, with the themes [in your essay].

I much agree with you that "the common core is attenuated, secularized, and trivial," and is not a base for building an institution. The question is how best to interpret the failure of the "common core" strategy. Was it a good idea, right while it lasted, which somebody betrayed, or a mistake whose weaknesses took time to work themselves out?

It could be a full-time professional occupation to watch and interpret the self-definition struggle around Notre Dame through the papers in the Hesburgh collection, through the series of "conversations on the Catholic character" which have run for the past two years...and all the rest of the discussion. It was probably unintentional (unintentional decisions are also revelatory) that the Hesburgh collection omits statements by persons who are informed and have been vocal on these issues for whom a Catholic use of the free-church alternative metaphor would be helpful (Shaffer, Hauerwas, myself, all of us having claimed to have something "catholic" to say). It does not include testimony of Catholics who believed that the content of Catholic (i.e. papal, conciliar, episcopal) social teaching should be prominent in the curriculum.... Visitors to the Kroc Institute for International Peace Studies are regularly astonished that the Theology Department does not even offer a course in "Catholic Social Teachings." The Hesburgh essay collection does not include anything from the long and munificent series of conferences directly on papal and episcopal documents managed from the Business College by [John] Houck and [Oliver] Williams.

When I watch the volume of people talking past each other, without moving toward concrete manageable resolutions of specific issues, I come to the hypothesis that "catholic" in this setting means something different from most of the above characterizations, yet also something very much at home within the Roman Catholic subculture. If you let people talk, the more the merrier, and keep the decisive cards close to the administrators' chest, nine-tenths of the critics will be satisfied by the fact that they are being encouraged to talk, and the decisive structures are stronger, not weaker, for the administration's not trying to control the debate or even enter it....

Conservative Protestants tend to think that what is wrong with "prelacy," whether in the diocese or in Rome, is that it is monarchical and the bishop can be intolerant. There have been reasons for that fear in the past. More weightily however, in many other settings, is the fact that a gentle and permissive bishop can implement a very tolerant inclusivism. Since 1983 the U.S. bishops have been backtracking on the principles riskily stated in <u>The Challenge of Peace</u>. Few bishops would stick their necks out to base serious management decisions on the touchy concerns you identify....[4] The first, lay meaning of "catholic," after all, is "inclusive." The problem may then be not that that the common core has become too thin, but that the outside shell has become porous.

It shows in some of the papers in the book that one profound change at Notre Dame is that the undergraduate student enters the University with no substantial understanding of or commitment to any substantially defined Catholic identity. When I began in 1967 Notre Dame undergraduates were literate; a sufficient critical mass had some Catholic cultural sensitivity from their youth in the parish or in Catholic schools. Now the freshman is illiterate. I see no clarity in the Hesburgh volume about what we should do about that. My hunch is that if that component of "Catholic identity" were solid, if the parishes were in fact producing Catholics, then the thinness of the common cultural core would not be as threatening on the level of how many faculty employees make an issue of their "freedom." Bethel College has less trouble staying by its conservative evangelical identity, because local evangelical churches are still producing pious kids. The diagnosis changes if we open the explanatory hypotheses to admit that the decisive changes in our world were not located in the University at all.

In other words, the spiritual/moral atmosphere in the University is a dependent variable, an index more than a causal factor. This does not make debates about how to be a Catholic school unimportant, but it might make them more modest. (To Robert E. Rodes, Jr., May 9, 1994)

A Footnote on the Value of Academic Discourse

Despite his habit of attending lectures and discussions all across campus,

---

[4]Rodes's paper listed four "political questions":

(1) Appointment of "people...whose teaching and scholarship support the transcendence of the human person" rather than nominal Catholics.

(2) Teaching so that students, after graduation, question "what effect their employers and associates are having at the margins of society, and ameliorate that effect as far as they can."

(3) Tenure and promotion decisions that "support the kind of intellectual enterprise we profess to desire" as distinguished from those "forms of peer review that look only at a candidate's achievements within some hermetic field of inquiry that excludes important aspects of the human and the real."

(4) Teaching and "research priorities" that "reflect a preferential option for the poor" as distinguished from those "that impress the biggest employers and the most important graduate schools.... To the point of exercising a preferential option for the rich."

John was not a big fan of academic discourse as an avenue to truthful insight. In a paper published in the Journal of Religious Ethics in 1996, commenting on Jeffrey Stout's widely read Ethics After Babel, John wrote: **"Academe differs from real moral communities of language in that the dimensions of promise-making and truth-telling, product quality and craftsmanship, which are present in every possible real human community, are less immediately effective in the university." In a footnote to that observation: "If the epistemological limits of academe were our theme, there would be more to say about the effects upon truth-finding of the odd ways in which universities are financed, whether by the state or by corporate deep pockets, and the way both integrity and flakiness are protected by unique institutions like tenure."**

The Central Focus in the "Religious Argument"
Discussion: Community

From my essay in the Journal of Legal Studies and from To Hear the Word:

Yoder was earnest and consistent about community, no more clearly so than when he took up Jesus's teaching about loving enemies and the injunction to decline the trappings of power in favor of servanthood. Jesus, Yoder said, was not talking about a commune or an eschatological utopia:

"The 'communitarians' of our time, for whom all meaning is internally self-authenticating...will not risk the challenge of telling the world that servanthood, enemy love, and forgiveness would be a better way to run a university, a town, or a factory. They pull back on the grounds that only they have already experienced the power and novelty of that threefold evangelical cord in the worship and ministry of the church. They affirm integrity but at the cost of witness."

Yoder quoted Dr. King: "When I took up the cross I recognized its meaning...," Dr. King said. "The cross may mean the death of your popularity. It may mean the death of a foundation grant. It may cut down your budget a little, but take up your cross, and just bear it. And that's the way I have decided to go." Yoder said that Jesus, when he talked about taking up the cross, was talking about "the specific punishment for insurrection. Followers of Jesus, he warns them, must be ready to be seen and to be treated as rebels, as was going to happen to him." And, of course, as happened to Dr. King.

Yoder studied under Karl Barth, and, apparently, with characteristic focus: Mr. Steinfels pointed out that Yoder gave Barth a fifty-page critique of Barth's teaching on pacifism, which he delivered to Barth on the day before Barth was to sit on Yoder's doctoral examination committee. John Yoder was a follower of Barth in proclaiming an alternative (biblical) legal order, a legal order that is universal, nonviolent, not coercive. **"(I)t cannot be imposed, only offered. It cannot be excluded by being declared to be alien, or 'private' or 'personal' or 'sectarian,' but**

only by not (i.e., not yet) being heard."

It is important to emphasize here that Yoder was talking about what Gerhard Lohfink described as a "contrast society." (He used that concept in To Hear the Word.) Yoder did not talk about individual righteousness very much. And, particularly in his politics and his jurisprudence, he did not talk about individual "rights" but about the witness of the community of faith. This was his politics and his jurisprudence because it was first of all his theology. **"Classical evangelical preaching," in its focus on the individual, is, he said, "too small an answer."** Specifically:

--The church needs to show that there are righteous ways in which power can be used.

--It needs to take account of the **"ethical insights, concerns, rights, and decisions of people who are not in power"** (perhaps meaning to point to the fact that only individuals have rights in American law).

--The mainline Christian church in America gives too much importance to coercive power and prestige: **"[I]f you place your hopes for the welfare of Italy and the glory of God in Italy on the conversion of Mussolini, you are no longer genuinely free to ask whether Fascism is wrong."**

--The mainline church **"dodges the fact, which a truly honest individual in a high position is very clear about, that many evils are matters of structure and not of inner disposition, so that the most unselfish heart in the world cannot necessarily 'use for good' or 'clean up' a fundamentally vicious structure."**

Yoder's jurisprudence points less to biblical principle than to a biblical process of community discernment: **"[T]here is a particular point where the redeemed individual and [the] social structure are both present, namely, in the Christian community as a visible body within history.... 'The primary social structure through which the gospel works to change other structures is that of the Christian community'"** (quoting The Politics of Jesus 153, 2nd ed.). Which is to argue that the Christian community is not only a model, a "contrast society," but also a resource; not only itself the biblical, ethical message but also itself an epistemology, a way to know and a way to know what to do--and, in both senses, probably, is heir to the Hebrew Prophets.

He argued that politics (and jurisprudence), taken up in the community of the faithful, will turn out both more reliable and more critical than politics (and jurisprudence) taken up in the civil community or in the nation-state. Beyond those marks of soundness, and more important than either of them, the community of the faithful is able to be experimental, where the civil community and the nation-state are not. The church, so understood, is **"a place where prophetic discernment is tested and confirmed, the organ for updating and applying the understanding of the revealed law of God, the context for the promised further guidance of the Spirit.... The church is both the paradigm and the instrument of the political presence of the**

gospel."

The church, understood as a discerning community, is able to be a place of deliberation, a paradigm for law and government, and the instrument of justice, because its processes give it credibility, and because it does not seek political or legal power: **"[T]he focus on the good guys getting control...becomes wrong...when control itself is seen as the goal and when power is seen as a neutral quantity easily usable for good.... [P]ower tends to corrupt; you need no theology to be more realistic than the American mood has been about 'government by the people' through their elected representatives.... [S]ervanthood is not a position of nonpower or weakness. It is an alternative mode of power...a way to make things happen...a way to be present. When we turn from coercion to persuasion, from self-righteousness to service, this is not a retreat but an end run. It brings to bear powers which, on balance, are stronger than the sword alone...truth rediscovered...the dissenter willing to suffer...the power of the people to withhold confidence...the attraction of an alternative vision...the integrity that accepts sacrifice rather than conformity to evil."**

To some extent, the advantage the church has as a community of discernment is that the church preserves and uses scripture. In <u>To Hear the Word</u>, John wrote of **"our renewed recourse to the original witnesses from the beginnings.... 'No creed but the Bible'...[means] we need to keep returning to them."** (Quotations from <u>To Hear the Word</u>, here and elsewhere in this book, are used with the permission of the publisher.) This has particular importance for those of us who "do" ethics:

The ministry of the ethicist is "professional" in the sense that some of the competences needed are technical, needing to be learned from and monitored by colleagues who also handle the data of intercultural, linguistic and conceptual arguments. But the ethicist is not <u>only</u> a professional. His or her service in explaining, transmitting, adjudicating the impact of the tradition are subject to the judgment of the believing congregation, most of whose members are not ethicists. She or he must make sense in ordinary language. This is not an insuperable difficulty, since (differing from at least some other ethical systems) the New Testament documents are also in ordinary language. (pp. 110-111)

John meant, when he wrote this way, to be talking about tangible, visible, earthy communities: **"Who is in high office or what laws are written will make less difference for many indices of where things will have gone...than the cumulation of an infinity of tiny deeds: mothers who feed their children, children who learn their lessons, craftsmen who finish a job, doctors who get the dosage right, drivers who stay on the road, policemen who hold their fire. The lunge for the large view is often the beginning of self-deception. The predilection to see one's own small deed as significant or as right when and because it can be shown to contribute to some overall victory scenario overburdens punctual responsibility in decision and** undervalues the continuities of character and covenant. The kingdom is like the grain growing while no one watches (Mark 4:26f), like the hidden leaven silently taking over the flour bin (Matt. 13:33). Contrary to the proverb, watching a pot does not keep it from boiling, but it does misdirect the pot watcher's creativity."

B. RELIGIOUS ARGUMENT IN CHURCH

I intend a note of irony in announcing that as the title of this second part of the first chapter of this book: What kind of argument might one expect in the church, if not religious argument? The point I learned from John Howard Yoder about this had to do with his experience in two relatively famous legal proceedings, one concerning Anabaptist school children, the other having to do with violence in Waco, Texas. John was interested in the sorts of arguments believers had to make, among themselves, on those cases.

On the criminal prosecution of the survivors of the 1994 Waco debacle, John felt, more than I did (and our going back and forth on it is an example of a religious argument in the church), that the church should <u>do</u> something:

The point would not be <u>only</u> to make an issue of the judicial process having gone wont, for which the judge and prosecutor are to blame (and perhaps shadowy federal administrators in the wings), but <u>through that</u> to ask about what went wrong previously and how so to define the issues, so that it is less likely to happen again, and fewer people are likely to want to sacrifice each other as defense against odd religions.

The "Committee for Waco Justice" has no standing. Am I right that the only people with standing now are those found guilty, and that the best way to meet the above objectives is to appeal those convictions? Or is there some bigger way to get hold of it? I remember a lifetime ago when a Lutheran minister in Michigan, whose reason for being involved I have never understood, asked me to serve on a "Committee for Amish Religious Liberty." Notre Dame sociology prof Leo Ward was also on it. What we did was wait until a likely family came up who were willing to be the test (turned out to be a Yoder in Wisconsin) and find them a lawyer (William Ball). The Committee itself did not litigate, but it prepared the rationale, helped choose the most fitting case, helped select the lawyer, provided moral support and kept the cause visible for all those years.

Would such a group make sense for this matter? It differs from the buildup to <u>Yoder v. Wisconsin</u>, in that the concern is not to make new law about religious liberty. (Or is it?) It is not just to scold the judge or the prosecutor, but to send a message to the Feds that this kind of disregard for ordinary citizens...is not acceptable. Would there be some point in having a group analogous to that one for this kind of concern? (Aug. 19, 1994)

Christians in Pluralist America

*From Religious Argument to Public Office and Then
to Responsibility for Results*

I had written in a draft something about the fate of the early 16th century Anabaptist reformers:
>The Anabaptists were slaughtered by the princes, often at the behest of the clergy, but not <u>by the Roman Catholic Church</u>.

"Not seek or accept civil office." If there was nonlethal civil office they did not reject it. Pilgram Marbeck was a civil engineer who most of his career was paid by city governments. The slogan "subject but not obedient" applies to "the sword," not to other things that might be called state.

John's translation of the key Schleitheim document, <u>The Legacy of Michael Sattler</u> 38 (1973):
>Thereby shall also fall away from us the diabolical weapons of violence–such as sword, armor, and the like, and all of their use to protect friends or against enemies–by virtue of the word of Christ: "you shall not resist evil."

Sattler does, though, appear to have also excluded offices that can <u>command</u> "the sword," such as that of magistrate or judge.

Schleitheim was February 1527. It can be argued that it took another decade for the normative vision of Schleitheim to trickle out, and the alternative visions to peter out, so that it is only after 1540 that most Anabaptists were normatively nonviolent (as distinguished from pragmatically powerless). But the position was there before Schleitheim....

In what sense did the justice of the law end on Calvary? Is this like the Lutheran Paul concerned for how to be justified? Or a [Rene] Girardian Paul saying that the retaliatory system is demoralized? Has there been no legal justice for 1,960 years?

When something about the American legal system is unjust, and you propose to make it better, in a way which your expertise and credentials enable you to suggest, would the result still not be the American legal system? (May 13, 1997)

Your contrasting the "gathered" church from the "witnessing" church [in discussing Steven Carter's book <u>The Culture of Disbelief</u>] is not a clean typology, in [the sense] that trueness to type would be a virtue. "Gathered" and "witnessing" are not disjunctive alternatives but ends of a scale for communities which accept not being in charge in a Christendom/Erastian way. Where a group lands on that scale may be partly something they can think about or decide upon, but mostly it is decided by the tyrants under whom they live. If the tyrants are relatively gentle, like London after the Glorious Revolution, then one can go as far toward the witnessing pole as Williams and Penn did, and actually take over a local government. But most of the time that option is excluded, not by the choice of the not-in-charge community. So where the minority finds itself on the gathered-to-witnessing scale is a dependent variable, not a theological choice.

It may become a theological choice, if, like the Amish or the Hasidim, some past experience of exclusion or persecution enters into the normative self-definition, and today's identity is always subject to being defined by past trauma; yet that backlash from repression is an eddy, not the stream. The Jews who since Jeremiah were called to "seek the peace of the city," and the Christians like Origen and Tertullian and Lactantius, who despite their non-violence claimed to be good citizens, do not fit the Amish-Hasidim paradigm and should not be thought of as deviations from it. They may be seen as showing people in the Amish backlash stance "that they should wade in more," but the Pennsylvania Dutch experience of "opting out" after the Quakers, who had given them religious freedom, and for whom they voted, were pushed out of the Pennsylvania Assembly, was not the Anabaptist paradigm.

Your letter points to another difference, namely "mainstream" people who discover some difference from Christendom, while still being mainstream. Even though some issues and some words are different, I don't see the types as congruent. "Mainstream" may be a purely quantitative designation; it is where most of the water runs. Or it may presume normative assumptions: (a) maybe that you have to please most people enough to get elected; or (b) maybe that your ethical requirement must not ask too much of ordinary non-heroic non-saintly people; or (c) maybe that your ethics if applied by everyone will not undercut the broadly Constantinian. These are different in detail, but all broadly Constantinian. They are not Erastian in the historical, technical sense of wanting the Queen to run the church, but they are Christendom in that the preachers consider their audience to be everyone. This is different from the preachers' or bishops' daring to state moral imperatives for the society which not everyone accepts, or which the present rulers do not accept. (Consider [The American Roman Catholic Bishops'] <u>The Challenge of Peace</u> on deterrence, or [President Bush's] Anglican bishop on the Gulf [War], or [discussion at Notre Dame] on what [Mario] Cuomo should do about abortion.[5])

---

[5]Governor Cuomo, in a talk at Notre Dame, affirmed his personal acceptance of the Catholic position on abortion (against) but made a distinction between himself as Catholic and himself as governor. Then, on the political and legal question, he took a "pro-choice" position. President Bush's Episcopalian bishop picketed outside the White House, against the Gulf War. The President invited him in, and they had a talk, at the end of which the President said he believed that war was a just war. The Bishop did not agree.

But as long as this dissenting normative guidance is non-binding, and is addressed to the public at large, I do not see these dissenting positions as proving they are "not as tied to America as they think they are," [a phrase I used in my essay on the Carter book]. Whether people in the inclusive churches "wade in" by being critical of the present government, and whether people from the "Anabaptist" (or Jeremian/Jewish) minorities "wade in," are quite different questions.

Part of being "the mainline church" in the simple descriptive sense is not having one center where thinking and deciding are done and identity is defined. That means that a statement like yours, "It discovers that it is not as tied to America as it thinks it is," floats in our minds. It is true of some people, and false of others. Those for whom it is true would give many different indices if you asked them how they now have discovered that, or whether it is good or bad to have lost the bond. (Jan. 20, 1994)

[To say] let religions try to impose their views, since the secularists do it, misses the important difference; when a secular power-bearer claims to be saving me he has to give reasons the whole polity can understand and vote on. [We were still talking–writing–about Shaffer on Carter.] He does not call on God to quiet his opposition. The secularist can be called to account. So can the theist who accepts the pluralistic policy. But not the theist who excludes his/her adversary from the hermeneutical circle. If I am the excluded adversary, I don't like the oppression. If I am a theologian, I don't like the abuse of the name of God.

I am not sure that believers should be obliged to make their moral claim in secular language, but neither should they have a right to a government-subsidized interpreter if they insist on doing it in Yiddish. If we really "seek the peace of the city," why should we fear that by saying our message in Babylonian we would have to destroy its meaning? Why should we not be able to translate? ... It is true that every statement in one language is unique and not absolutely translatable. It is also true that between any two linguistic cultures a moderately bilingual person can produce a functionally adequate equivalent in one language of what you said in the other. I'd rather be asked to learn to talk democratic-secular than Irish-Catholic.

I agree that my primary frame of reference is the people of God, but it does not follow that I have no concern for the civil society. That concern is derivative, but it is real. I'd rather have [a civil society] where potholes get fixed than one where they don't. [Your] "morally inert like the weather" is not a good metaphor [for the government]. Floods and tornadoes are not inert; but <u>that</u> is not what is wrong with the metaphor. One can change government; the religiously farthest out of the Fathers, Williams and Penn, did the most to make American polity viable. One can change government best if one is most independent of it. The position which cannot change government is the Erastian. (Dec. 9, 1993)

Moral Memoranda From John Howard Yoder

On "Soft Pluralism"

"A soft pluralism, when consistent, provides the most livable cultural space for Jews and Anabaptists, as well as for Jehovah's Witnesses and followers of Rev. Moon," John wrote in an essay in the <u>Journal of Religious Ethics</u>, in 1996. "As a <u>civil</u> arrangement, pluralism is better than any of the hitherto known alternatives. As an ecclesiastical arrangement, it is better than the monarchical episcopate. As a marketplace of ideas, it is better than a politically correct campus or a media empire homogenized by salesmanship. For such reason, Stanley Hauerwas's characterization of English-speaking justice as a set of 'bad ideas' strikes me as too simple."

When he provided (unpublished) comments on papers by Professor Steven Pepper, at Georgetown, in April 1989, John made it clear, though, that he understood, as well as constitutional lawyers do, that the arrangement he preferred is a matter more of power overlooked than of power recognized, and that the arrangement as we have it is not exactly consistent: **"The American government does have a place for intermediate associations, but only with a certain embarrassment.... It is easier for American thought to assume a vacuum of vested rights between the individual and the state, conceding status to groups only when individuals create ad hoc associations in order to hold a meeting, own a meetinghouse, or do good works. Yet paradoxically, we still find that legislative ascription of exemptions can be given more easily to subculture groups than to conscientious individuals."**

In <u>Nevertheless: Varieties of Religious Pacifism</u> (1992), John wrote: **"Power, even if it be called 'coercive,' is of a personal, humane kind as long as the individuals toward whom it is directed are conceived of as persons and their life is protected.... The power of office in business, school, or church, or even in nonlethal state functions, can be disciplined by the objectives of those institutions."**

Yoder on the Politics of Necessary Evil

[Whoever uses] the aphorism..."to have clean hands is to have no hands"...is assuming that moral responsibility is best described in terms of the avoidance of dirt. That itself is as I see it a Puritan or nomistic way to conceive of morality. Certain acts are forbidden, one assumes; yet to be effective one must commit them. Ergo, dirt is unavoidable.

What if the avoidance of the forbidden were not the right way to describe right being, deciding, and doing? Gospel ethics is not guided by the avoidance of the prohibited:

"Nothing is forbidden but not everything is useful; I will not let anything enslave me." (I Cor. 6:12.) "Nothing is forbidden; but not everything is useful; not

everything helps the building to grow."

[Reinhold] Niebuhr never believed in personal anguished choice. He was not bothered by close personal casuistry. He rather updated Luther's "pecca fortiter" into "do with a good conscience the deed which although sinful is realistically likely to produce the least evil results." He made that a social, not just a personal duty. He brought to the advocacy of this lesser evil deed the moral passion of his Reformed background, unchanged from his Social Gospel days. You don't found two periodicals and write a dozen books if "anguish" is your last word about political decision. That no-one's-hands-are-clean became for him a positive argument in favor of a political ethic of unashamed (although avowedly ambivalent) national interest. (Feb. 22, 1989)

Moral discernment asks not how to be blameless but how to represent in the world the servanthood of Jesus. In a fallen world, that "weakness" will always include the inability to prevent some evil's happening, and in [Reinhold] Niebuhr's terms that means participation in guilt. So be it, in those terms. The "sin" of not being able to prevent crucifixion is preferable to the "sin" of killing. Yet the avoidance of "sin" is the least nuanced way to say it.

I do not deny that civil law and the management of institutions must have their bottom threshold of the forbidden; but it is wrong to let those concerns dictate our primary affirmative paradigms. If the affirmative paradigm of not breaking the rules is wrong, then Niebuhr's argument based upon it (anyone who acts has dirty hands) is also inappropriate. His argument that, since Gandhi and Hitler both cause [violence], therefore the avoidance of violence is an amoral impossibility, is intellectual sleight of hand, not serious argument.... (Feb. 22, 1989)

John's deepest anthropological disagreement with Reinhold Niebuhr, I think, is communal, as in The Royal Priesthood, p. 19, reprinted from an essay in the April 1955 Mennonite Quarterly Review: "(T)he body of Christ differs from other social bodies in that it is not less moral than its individual members. If being a perfectly loyal American, a freemason, or a bourgeois identifies a man with that group egoism in such a way as to make him less loving than he would be as an individual, the contrary is true of being a member of Christ. Thus the thesis of Moral Man and Immoral Society falls down in the crucial case, the only one which is really decisive for Christian ethics."

Yoder on Powell's Unremarkable Communitarianism

When "Augustinian" means a neoplatonic or a Constantinian reason for relativizing Jesus I consider Augustine wrong. When "Augustinian" means an awareness of the pervasiveness of pride in fallen power structures I am with [H. Jefferson] Powell. If democracy is more revisable (in the direction of relativizing prideful power and helping the underdog) than the alternatives are, I would prefer it. If a judge with tenure is more likely to respect the underdog and the outsider than is one pandering to an imminent majoritarian democratic election, than that deference for the minority...seems preferable.

But most of Powell's book [The Moral Tradition of American Constitutionalism, 1993] is on other subjects, and most of my response would not be drawn from that ancient text of mine [that Powell used to evaluate the tradition]....[6]

First I would ask you as historian whether his history is correct. Although theologically aware all the time, Powell does not bring in as much theology as your blurb [an invitation to John to speak at a conference on Powell's book] suggests....

The primary theme with which Powell begins is not theology as such, or the particular theological accent he borrows from me at the end, but the thesis that in the chaos of many different ways to read the story of constitutionalism, the generally MacIntyrean vision of community-borne meanings is more able to tell the story adequately than are the others. I take it you appreciate that, which does not surprise me; but is arguing that the theme of your event? Powell observes (I think rightly) that the aptness of the MacIntyrean style is independent of theology, in the way [Alasdair] MacIntyre argued before he reverted to Christianity, and certainly quite independently of his narrowing his Christian loyalty into his own brand of Thomism. The rightness of MacIntyre's observing that all meaning is community-borne, and of Powell's taking that over, is like the rightness of observing that what I have been writing all my life is prose. Very true, but so what? Citing MacIntyre to say that meaning is community-dependent is like citing Kuhn to say that paradigms shift. It is so obviously the agreed wisdom that it will seldom throw new light on some contested issue. (January 22, 1996)

In Conclusion: Two Jurisprudential Issues:
(i) The Source and Reason for Legal Argument
and (ii) The Processes for Making It

From my Journal of Legal Studies essay: That raises two jurisprudential issues of some interest. One of these is the source of and reason for political and legal argument. The other is the process by which that source and reason are

---

[6]John and I participated in a "conversation" on Powell's book, in March 1996 at Notre Dame. It was published as "H. Jefferson Powell on the American Constitutional Tradition: A Conversation," 72 Notre Dame Law Review 11 (1996). John led the first session with an extended, prepared statement (in the published version, at 27-28).

connected to the concrete issues on which believers speak to the civil community and to the nation-state.

Source and Reason. There is such a thing as a biblical jurisprudence. In The Politics of Jesus, Yoder took issue with Christian theologians who taught that Jesus of Nazareth did not have a political (and legal) agenda. There is a social agenda in the New Testament, as John read scripture, which is both substantive and procedural.

The substantive agenda is:

–that the regime recognize the dignity of each of its members and all of its members–male and female, Jew and gentile, slave or free;

–that the regime be capable of practicing, and in fact practice, forgiveness ("Social scientists call it conflict management");

–that the regime practice justice in a radical, biblical sense, so that "there will never be any poor among you" (Deuteronomy 15:3, N.E.B.);

–that the results of public discourse give influence to each of its members, as (to invoke the Pauline metaphor) each part of the human body has its irreplaceable function.

This substantive agenda is open to argument, but it is also the constitution of what the German theologian Gerhard Lohfink called a "contrast society." The local community of believers can, more readily than the civil community or the nation-state, put this agenda into practice, as its law. Its persuasive office in the secular community is carried out as it does so, and as it is seen to do so. It is plausible that a community of believers can practice equality, equal dignity, forgiveness, and reconciliation, not only because that is the sort of community it wants to be, but in order to instruct the secular society around it. **"The church is called to live, and is beginning to live (to the extent to which we get the point), in the way to which the whole world is called." (46) "[T]here is no reason to want to make sense to your neighbors if you have no identity worth sharing with them"....**

In making contrasts such as the comparison of the mainline church with congregations in the Black Church, Yoder spoke mainly of Christians. But he was beginning to develop an historical theology around a radical Judaism that would reach from the Prophet Jeremiah, to the series of events that led to the separation of Jewish Christianity from early rabbinic Judaism, to what Rabbi Joseph Solovietchik spoke of as Jewish involvement in all of humankind's modern confrontation with the cosmos. As nearly as I can tell, Yoder did not get as far with this project as he would have liked; in any case, one of the sad results of his death is that we do not have a fuller development of his reverence for Judaism.

In For the Nations, he recognized that Christian moral standards "derived from, and [are] therefore...fruitfully illuminated by, older Jewish models of how to relate to this world's powers." In his description of what he called "the

Moral Memoranda From John Howard Yoder

Jeremianic Model":

--There is no need to seize power. God is sovereign over history.

--The "ultimate righteous social order" is the business of the Messiah.

--Efforts (other efforts) to establish a national kingship are not blessed by God. "It is not only that the Maccabees and the Zealots did not ultimately triumph. Their first successes led them to become oppressive and to fall out among themselves. Not because they were weak but because they were strong and 'succeeded,' they fell prey to what they claimed to defeat."

In what Yoder described as the "Mosaic project," the captivity of the Jews in Babylon and the destruction of the first Temple were not a parenthesis; they were a beginning "under a firm, fresh prophetic mandate," to witness to the nations, "to retrieve the heritage of the centuries during which the people of God discharged their mission without being in charge of the world."

The life and witness and teachings of the rabbi Jesus were continuous with this Mosaic project. "[T]he Gospel account affirms a sequence of historic projects in which precursor and successors both understand God to be working in the real world to establish justice." Neither the gospels nor the rabbis reduced religion to ethics, as the American Social Gospel did. The Jeremianic model proclaimed "new social possibility for the human story," and, I think, a new jurisprudence as well. "The community [Jesus] creates is the product and not the enforcer of that new regime. His followers will live from, not toward the victory of Christ. Our life is to proclaim, not to produce, the new world." Which, as to Yoder's developing theory about Judaism, is to say that, for Jesus, there was not a new social goal; his social goal was the Mosaic social goal.

This Jewish and Christian theological social ethic is precisely <u>legal</u>: "We are not called to make the bread of the world available to the hungry; we are called to restore the true awareness that it always was theirs. We are not called to topple the tyrants, so that it might become true that the proud fall and the haughty are destroyed. It already is true; we are called only to let that truth govern our own choice of whether to be, in our turn, tyrants claiming to be benefactors." Law, then (and this shows how he took issue with Reformation jurisprudence), is a form of grace.

He took issue as well with Catholic natural-law politics and jurisprudence: "[W]hen the 'nature of things' is properly defined, the organic relationship to grace is restored. The cross is not a scandal to those who know the world as God sees it, but only to the pagans, who look for what they call wisdom, or the Judaeans, who look for what they call power.... [T]he choice of Jesus was ontological: it risks an option in favor of the restored vision of how things really are. It has always been true that suffering creates shalom. Motherhood has always meant that. Servanthood has always meant that. Healing has always meant that. Tilling the soil has always meant that. Priesthood has always meant that. Prophecy has always meant that. What Jesus did...was that he renewed the definition of kingship to fit with the priesthood and prophecy. He saw that the suffering servant is king as much as he is priest and prophet. The cross is neither foolish nor weak, but natural."

John saw his own thought as a sort of dialogue between scripture and what Vatican II called "the signs of the times." Much of To Hear the Word deals with the way he read scripture when he did this. For example, this discussion of St. Paul's speaking of angels and of principalities and powers:

"The work of Christ has an impact upon that cosmos. Christian interpretation since medieval times has assumed that this was repeating something about 'angels' which we already knew and has therefore paid little further attention to those texts. Scholastic Protestantism gave them still less attention. Liberal Protestantism consciously excised them from its practical canon, knowing that they describe something which we already know cannot be, namely, a world of familiar spirits behind the causation of events. As a result, a major segment of Paul's understanding of the universe and of redemption has been made inoperative.

"A series of Reformed theologians–Berkhof, Caird, Morrison, Markus Barth, and others–have revitalized our awareness of the relevance of this material. When I drew from them in a secondary synthesis in one chapter of my Politics of Jesus, there were those who felt it to be an inappropriate expression of my Mennonite bias, even though all of the sources I used, both the scriptural and the systematic theologians, were consistently in the Reformed tradition. But my present concern is not that my reading was Reformed, but that it was new, yet old. The text was always there, but a new age opened our eyes to read it. This has been happening throughout the centuries, at least since St. Francis if not since Augustine. Scriptural orientation sharpens the ability to discern the signs of the times, but it is just as true that temporal orientation sharpens our ability to discern the signs in Scripture. This is a concrete case, in our age, of the fulfillment of the promise of which the puritan John Robinson has spoken: 'The Lord has yet more light and truth to break forth....'

"It is most lively and productive to think of one body of literature, the Bible, representing in any time and place the testimony of the narrative stretching from Abraham to the Apostles, which can be juxtaposed to any other age by its psalms being sung again, its letters being read again, its stories and parables being retold. Then, in the juxtaposition of those stories with our stories there leaps the spark of the Spirit, illuminating parallels and contrasts, to give us the grace to see our age in God's light and God's truth in our words. This picture of how it works is more representative of the experienced facts, but also more rigorous than the classical scholastic vision of an unchanging body of timeless propositions needing to be twisted to fit a new age by the special skills of

Moral Memoranda From John Howard Yoder

rationalistic linguists." (pp. 78-79)

Chapter Two

War, Peace, Lethal State Power, and Legal Ethics

Chapter One dealt mostly with what John worked out on the traditional Anabaptist issue of withdrawal from civic life. As Mr. Steinfels's obituary noticed (quoted here in the Preface), John was both unusual among Anabaptists and forthright in his dissent from the tradition of withdrawal. Particularly in the last years of his life, he built a theology of involvement from what Jeremiah wrote to Judah in exile in Babylon ("seek the peace of the city") that was, as I think of it, remarkable.

In this Chapter Two I have attempted to gather material on what I think of as the second principal issue in Yoder on the law. That is the issue of obedience to power. That, too, is a traditional Anabaptist issue: The radical reformers in Zurich in the early 16th century went to their deaths because they dissented from Christendom and distinguished between membership in the Kingdom of God and what the post-Enlightenment world has talked of (reviving an ancient Greek notion) as citizenship. This issue has particular bite for a lawyer who is also a believer, and especially so among lawyers in the United States, where we take an oath to obey the state and are sternly directed in our regulatory rules to tell our clients to obey the law. That civil apparatus, as John noticed in a paper given in North Park, Illinois, in 1990, has a way of becoming an ethic....

I found in John's files a manuscript entitled "Ethics and Eschatology," a paper that had been given in what he identified as the "North Park Symposium," in October, 1990. It was published in a journal called Ex Auditu (volume six) and is used, here and in Chapter Three, with permission. I refer to it here as "North Park,

1990." What follows is excerpted from the manuscript in John's file, is only a small part of it, and omits John's footnotes. This comes as close as anything I know about to expressing John's jurisprudence.

A. ETHICAL GROUNDWORK

[Consider] the providential place of the power-bearer.... It is assumed, at least since Eusebius, that the frame of reference of ethical deliberation is that of the person with power: the king deciding whether to wage an unjust war, the merchant deciding whether to set a fair price, the head of household deciding whether to beat his wife or his child, the wealthy person deciding whether to lend at interest. The action is to be evaluated not by whether it keeps the rules, or by whether it resonates with the grace of God, or by whether it exemplifies virtue, or whether it coheres with the salvation story, but by whether, when carried out, when generalized through the ruler's power, it will produce the best possible outcomes.

Modern analysts of moral logic call this "consequentialism," the moral validation of a choice or an action by its results. Ethical theory can analyze its self-evident strengths and its less obvious weaknesses. What we seldom analyze is the sitz in leben of consequentialism. Evaluating means by ends is only self-evident when two assumptions obtain: (a) that the social system of causation is a transparent nexus of connections, comparable to a machine whose shafts and cogwheels interact in reliable ways, so that the results of one's decision and action can be calculated; and (b) that the actor whose decision we are evaluating has power.

We are seldom reminded that these two assumptions (actually three, as we shall soon see) obtain, even for us, only seldom and very imperfectly. The sociopolitical nexus is by no means subject to exhaustive analysis as a machine, when there are multiple actors, some of whom have a stake in interfering with one another's intentions or denying one another's rights. Neither the social scientist nor the politician really knows what will in fact result from this or that choice. Even the historian, after the fact, is at a loss in the face of some major events to "explain" why what in fact happened.

I was one of a tableful of faculty colleagues privileged to host at Notre Dame, early in 1989, the first sociologist from the Soviet Union to visit our university. We plied him with questions about whether perestroika was going to work. He answered that it was not within his competence to say, since the sociologist is a scientist, and scientists deal with what can be generalized and replicated. Michael Gorbachev not only cannot be replicated; he cannot be explained. In terms of social science, he could not have happened. Politics is the art of the possible; history on the other hand is the realm of the unique, sometimes the impossible.

The first characteristic I ascribed to consequentialistic reasoning was its assumptions about causation. Secondly, it makes important assumptions about information, which are a part of the causation picture, but constitute an independent source of uncertainty. In order to make decisions on the basis of preferable outcomes, one must know the facts of the case, exhaustively and accurately. There may be simple settings where such highly accurate knowledge exists, about what will be the outcome if I do this instead of that; but hardly can that obtain if I do this instead of that; hardly can that obtain in modern social conflicts. Some facts are so complex as to be unknowable; some are the object of secrecy, or of disinformation.

A third characteristic of consequential justifications of actions, the one I began with, is the assumption that the actor disposes of power, so that he or she or they can in fact "make a difference." The Western experience of ethics is inseparable from the assumption that the behavior whose rightness one seeks to illuminate is that of the bearers of power. If someone challenges the morality of violence, the counterquestion is: "Should we disarm the police? Should Churchill have let Hitler overrun the world?" If the question is the sacredness of fetal life, the "strong" answer is the one declaring abortion a crime. Rulers are the prototypical moral agents; if an act is immoral it must be sanctioned civilly. If the rulers do not punish an act, it is "condoned," i.e. not <u>really</u> wrong.

Other Moral Reasoning

Fifteen years ago I was visiting a small Roman Catholic theological seminary in South Africa, discussing the moral resources for nonviolent social struggle, a vision which was born in that country in the work of Gandhi. One of the students immediately appealed to the action of John F. Kennedy in the 1962 Cuban missile crisis, as having proven the rightness of armed conflict. What is striking is not the status of the arguments for or against violence, or for or against the American policies of 1962, but the assumption made by a poor black man in South Africa that the settings in which the President of the United States makes decisions are more paradigmatic than his own. Even the weakest of us would rather daydream about what they would do if they were President than struggle with what to do at the bottom of the pile.

Apocalyptic and prophetic literature does us the service of ignoring and thereby striking down our confidence in system-immanent causal explanations for the past, and, even more, in system-immanent causal descriptions of how the future is sure to unfold from the choice we are just now making. It reminds us of a world view in which the cosmos was not all knowable; where transcendence could be expressed in terms of divine (or demonic) agency without the real world, rather than being restricted to some other dimension. That frees us for the possibility that other than consequential modes of moral reasoning--founded for instance in virtue, in motivations in obedience to <u>halakah</u>–not subject to being set aside on sequentialist grounds, might be admitted.

The specific "other moral reasoning" that is the most evident is <u>hope</u>. When we make the ancient world an odd subset of our own, the strangeness of the literature of "vision" is easily classified in terms of social or psychological pathology. It is explained as compensating for weakness, fear, and defeat. It can be compared to schizophrenia; one reads of "culture shock" and "social powerlessness" as explanations. Parallels can be sought in the "ghost dances" which signaled the breakdown of the original American culture, or the "cargo cults" which arise on the frontier between traditional and imperial culture in Africa or Southeast Asia. Such comparisons to modern pathologies are not utterly erratic, but they do not capture what was essential to the biblical seers. The odd visions generally cited from our century as approximate analogies seldom render their communities more viable. The biblical seers were not compensating for desperation--at least they did not say they were. They said they were engaging in doxology, restating in a new setting their proclamation of the resurrection. They were testifying that the powers of oppression were swallowed up in God's larger story, whereas our modern explanations try to do it the other way around, by subsuming God talk in our own visions of human dignity and therapy.

"Be faithful unto death; I will give you the crown of life." "Faithfulness" in this setting included for the beleaguered first-century believers much that we would call "ethical" by way of truth-telling, promise-keeping, sexual purity, et cetera; yet the primordial ethical obligation is the cohesion of the believing community in the face of the pressures working against its identity. Sometimes those pressures pushed toward dilution of identity from inside through schism or speculation. Sometimes they threatened destruction from outside through banishment or martyrdom. In either case the first imperative is to discern the temptation to deny the faith, and not to yield to it. The strategies of identity maintenance which we may call "exclusiveness" when we see them in a modern sect have a different meaning in a clandestine synagogue. The claim to be the only bearers of truth, which is ecumenical bad manners in our pluralistic and tolerant setting, is a simple fact. In your eyes, your survival is the only way for the honor of the only true God to be upheld in your corner of Asia Minor.

But it is not enough to affirm the value of survival; death too is a part of victory. The crucifixion of Jesus, described by the evangelists as model for the readiness of his disciples to suffer, is transmuted in the first vision of John into the sovereignty of the slain lamb as key to the cosmic mystery. The reason John is told not to weep is that the death of the lamb has purchased a new people to share in His reign; they share in the stoic sense of internal dignity, the integrity of the one who can keep "hanging in there" whatever the cost; it is in fact what moves the world....

It is not false when people who call themselves "realists," from Machiavelli to Klausewitz to Reinhold Niebuhr, tell us that power comes from the barrel of a gun. That is one kind of power. It is not that the seers compensate for their being in fact incapacitated, by dreaming vindictively about cosmic catastrophe; it is that to be disarmed after the mode of Christ is to be endowed with the power of truth-telling (recently renamed "consciousness-raising") and community-building, for which the metaphors of cosmic conflict are most apt because they break the frame of normalcy.[7] [North Park, 1990]

Oaths

What does it mean to swear to "support" the constitutions of California and of the U.S.A.?

The fact that the meaning of the verb is not defined [in, for example, the California oath for lawyers] so that the layman can know what he is being obliged to commit to is part of the reason not to make the commitment. I can promise to <u>submit</u> to the provisions of the Constitution, to the extent which they apply to me, since/if/because I know they are tolerable, and because my nonviolent commitment means I am ready to suffer injustice. To <u>support</u> may by the readings of some mean <u>obey</u> or <u>implement</u> and that makes it more uncertain how I am to know what I am being asked to promise.[8]

I suspect that many, most lay people and some lawyers, would say that the submission which is wanted is that in principle I give the constitutional government a blank check. Any blank check is prima facie suspect as potential idolatry. The principle that counts is that the believer and not the ruler must judge as to what is compatible with the believer's loyalty to the only true God.

Further, it has not been assured constitutionally that the government

---

[7] I am not arguing that the Christian must avoid being in a position of power, nor that there is nothing to say about how rulers behave.... What I reject is (a) considering the ruler as the primordial mover of history, and (b) modifying the content of moral obligation in order to approve of the ruler's doing things which would be wrong for others. [North Park, 1990]

[8] The federal constitution, Art. II, Sec. 1, mandates an oath for the president that requires her or him to "preserve, protect and defend the constitution." The Indiana constitution, art. 15, sec. 4, requires public officers to swear that they will "support the Constitution of this State, and of the United States." Lawyers' oaths are typically of the latter sort.

cannot order me to kill. The Bill of Rights supports the free exercise of religion, but since administrations have made arrangements for C.O. exemption the issue of refusing military service has not been defined as a free exercise right,[9] as I have written in my papers in your field, with no one contradicting me. Any organization that claims the right to make me shed blood for it, i.e. perform at its behest the most basic forbidden cultic act, is an idol. (September 19, 1994)

B. JUST WAR

A focus for thinking about the lethal power of law has been just-war theory, a subject that never wanders out of sight on John's and my campus, and one that became prominent during the Viet Nam War, again during the Gulf War, and most recently during President George W. Bush's "war" on terrorism. In the earlier two instances, both John and I coped with the law of conscription. My impression–I wrote John–was that the drift in liberal opinion has been toward finding just-war doctrine (to use the provocative word) useless, and in fact not used seriously by either lawyers or their apologists: There never seems to be an unjust war, I wrote. Both John and I, as I recall, were thinking of a probing, learned lecture, given by my law-school colleague the late Father William M. Lewers, C.S.C., on just war; what I said to John about the "doctrine" came, in my own words, from what Father Lewers said. The point had daily legal significance as lawyers in our community sought, with casuistry and mildly insincere legal argument, conscientious-objector status for young Roman Catholic clients. John was characteristically selective:

I would be interested in knowing what you would do next with your insight that "the just war tradition is not useful for a Christian." What you say about "just war" would seem to me to be applicable to most of the rest of "the law"; yet you stay in the guild. We need a language and a casuistry for continuing to work with the way things are, after having seen that the self-justifications they proclaim for themselves are not water-tight, just as [Reinhold] Niebuhr needed to explain why to commit the "right sin" (as to war, not even under just-war limits), rather than the wrong sin of pacifist irresponsibility.

I am not sure [referring to an analogy of mine, that just-war theory is like a beautiful horse that nobody rides] a farm boy should have disgust for a beautiful horse no one could harness; one can admire its beauty, as one does of the trees one

---

[9]That is, conscientious objection is not a first-amendment constitutional right. When John wrote "Administrations," I believe he was referring to the Selective Service Act, which is where the statutory right of conscientious objection comes from.

does not cut and the cathedrals in which one does not pray. Just don't justify the horse on the ground that it can be ridden. Don't claim to be riding it when you aren't. Most people who say the just-war system can't work are realists or crusaders who want less restraint. The [Catholic Bishops'] 1983 pastoral is better than that. If Notre Dame R.O.T.C. students took that as a guide, our alumni would kill fewer people....

I am interested in integrity. People who claim casuistic honesty for a method of making exceptions which really have to be justified by rules for exception-making, and don't just begin a slippery slide, should be tested by that.... I don't think my critique of others' insufficient integrity is refuted by my not winding it up with the right answer.... [I]f people structure their discourse about discipleship differently, it is wrong to squeeze them through the rules-and-exceptions grid and make them legalists.

If "responsibility" is a relationship of owing an accounting to someone, I rejoice in people who see the human situation that way. That could be what you call "not evasive." For Reinhold Niebuhr (more bluntly than for H. Richard), that term, however, has much more narrow content, namely the obligation to intervene in the power game, to help history turn out right. Its counterpart vice, irresponsibility, is the sin of pacifists. As long as H.R.N. keeps the concept more formal, fine; but it gets more muddled if we move from stating a relationship to defining what one should do and why. (June 21, 1995)

Doubt About Law As Conversation

When you distinguish between the law as a discipline and the government as an institution, for instance when contrasting Lutherans and Calvinists, I could wish for that distinction to be pursued more deeply. Bob Rodes, with his broad dialogical vision of the law as a community conversation,[10] seems to me to slight the fact that people who promulgate positive regulations do so usually not as generous instruments of unselfish consensus but as tyrants, whose selfishness is mitigated only by the extent to which historical processes of struggle have brought them under some discipline by their subjects. (May 20, 1995)

---

[10]Notably in Rodes's little jurisprudence book, The Legal Enterprise (1976). The notion is also implicit throughout his three-volume study of the English establishment and in his two books on liberation theology, as well as in two articles: "Law, Social Change and the Ambivalence of History," Proceedings of the American Catholic Philosophical Association 164 (1975), and "A Prospectus for a Symbolist Jurisprudence," 2 Natural Law Forum 88 (1957). A full list of Rodes's publications (as of 1998) appears at 73 Notre Dame Law Review 769-772.

Moral Memoranda From John Howard Yoder

The Provisional Legitimacy of the Law

There is no civil order that is not subject to the Risen Lord Seated at the Right Hand of the Father. But the mode of the several principalities and powers being subject is that of rebellious creatures, sometimes more and sometimes less effectively being tamed and sometimes breaking their leashes. They are not subject the way a private does what the sergeant says....

My claim is that the patience of the suffering servant with the rebellious world concedes to those structures <u>even though rebellious</u> a measure of provisional legitimacy and even interim usefulness, including yielding to them when they kill him, and empowering them to keep sometimes a relative "peace" like the <u>Pax Romana</u>, or like the way the U.S.S.R. and Yugoslav dictators prevented genocide. (May 1, 1993)

"Certainly any renunciation of violence is preferable to its acceptance," John wrote in <u>The Politics of Jesus</u>, "but what Jesus renounced is not first of all violence, but rather the compulsiveness of purpose that leads men to violate the dignity of others." (p. 244)

On Being a Christian and a Lawyer

I am interested that you will be speaking soon to a group of Mennonite lawyers.... I suspect you will be surprised to discover their attitude, which is complicated by complexes derived from the ghetto experience of a religious minority. You will find that many of them are apologetic about the impossibility of reconciling faithfulness with effectiveness, and feel that if they are to be active out in the real wild world they would rather be guided by Niebuhr than by Jesus. (April 16, 1987)

John might have advised–or warned–me that that fascinating group of Christian lawyers formed a community that was (and, I suppose, is) capable of discussing and discerning how a non-violent Christian lawyer should go about pursuing her or his craft. Some of those present did only office practice. Some went to court but represented only defendants. Some pursued a broader litigation practice but made broader moral judgments about their clients' purposes–broader judgments than the American adversary ethic would require of them.

I wonder whether "lawyering" is so univocal that one could or should decide, in the terms in which you set it up, "I as a Christian must be a lawyer" or "I must not." Writing wills and contracts so as to be easy to implement, defending poor widows against the housing authority, defending people against capital punishment, prosecuting, judging, postponing the implementation of environmental rules, structuring corporate mergers leveraged with junk bonds, are all lawyering, but they are not all the same morally.

War, Peace, Lethal State Power, and Legal Ethics

Instead of, "Am I as a Christian called to be a lawyer?" would not the question, "Which of the things that lawyers do is a follower of Jesus called to do?" be a more discriminating and manageable question? If either my friends in the guild or my brothers and sisters in the church want to help me discern, would that not be what they would do? Although in ultimate moral accountability, you (following William Stringfellow) refused in principle to sell out morally to any less-than-divine Lord, you do begin with an epistemological absolute, i.e., that the concept "lawyer" is univocal.... [No I don't!]

In real life there are notions already built into the culture, there are events, there are institutions, there are persons, there are the factual data of the material world, each of these dimensions being meaningful in terms of the others. Reality is multidimensional, just as is the hermeneutics of peoplehood. Rodes thinks that the concepts are self-exegeting under the heading of "nature," while you think that the stories are self-privileged, capable of freeing the dialog from the relativity and vulnerability of actually listening, talking, and deciding. From where I stand, when Rodes says "nature is univocal" and you seem to say "story is univocal," although your answers are different your methods seem to me both to make the same prior mistake, and in both cases the thesis loses me, leaving me to ask "but what if it does not say that to me?" The univocality claim in either case leaves me out of the loop. (July 31, 1995)[11]

[After I learned that lesson:] "You want to distinguish qualitatively between saying, "A Christian cannot be a soldier" (as the early church disciplines did, although we don't know how they were applied) and saying, "A Christian might be a lawyer, but there are some kinds of lawyering she would not do." Until you explain more, I have to say the difference is only quantitative, depending on how many of the components of lawyering or soldiering (in a specific setting) are incompatible with following Jesus. If "the barrier is put up in front of the category," that can be a wise pastoral advice without its moral claims being

---

[11]The reference to Rodes is to his account of natural law, which, in this reference, is a matter of consulting nature for guidance in knowing what is going on (and therefore in ethics); what John was talking about here is not in my view wildly different from the account other modern natural-law jurisprudes would give. The reference to my use of stories is to a narrative theory that is discussed elsewhere in this book (Chapter Three). John's reference to his own "hermeneutics of peoplehood" is significant since it forms his own approach to what Rodes would find in nature and I in stories; it refers to the scripture-governed deliberations of the congregation of believers; that phrase was the title of an article in The Journal of Religious Ethics (Spring 1982) which became the first chapter in John's book The Priestly Kingdom (1984).

dependent on needing to prove just how many things normally done in the category are wrong. Stringfellow's point [when he said he was not a member of the legal profession, but was a biblical person working in the law] was to relativize his lawyering, being only his job, whereas, in the arguments I care about, the point is to affirm the autonomy of the "vocation" as a moral guide, including duties different from discipleship. (Aug. 16, 1995)

The Moral Force of the Words "Legal" and "Power"

[I had titled a draft essay "Faith Subverts Legal Order." Among many useful suggestions, John persuaded me to change the title to "Faith Tends to Subvert Legal Order."[12]] If by "legal order" you mean some people are wealthy, then the Gospel message is subversive. If "legal order" means some people are armed--ditto. If the "legal order" is the princes--ditto. But why accept that definition of "legal order"? Couldn't a legal order still be a legal order and say the poor should be fed? Or that hospitals should care for the sick poor? Or that children should learn to read?

It is only with a particular "fallen" definition of what the "order" has to be recognized as, that the only contribution for the Christian to make is subversion. There are those who define "civil order" as only the monopoly of violence, and there are places where that is all that is going on. But in other places or times justice would be done; that would not make the order less "civil" or "legal."

When something about the American legal system is unjust, and you propose to make it better, in a way which your expertise and credentials enable you to suggest, would the result not still be the American legal system? ... My ecclesiology is quite analogous to that of Jews from Jeremiah to Hertzl; of them what you say about "subversion," as a byproduct of faithfulness, rather than an end in itself, would run in parallel. (Nov. 5, 1997)

There is a very deep and confusing ambivalence in the term "powerlessness"... A few hours after...you characterized Jesus as "powerless," I heard Colman McCarthy saying, "I am a pacifist, because I believe in force, the force of ideas...." Both "power" and "force" can be used in a basic etymological sense, meaning simply the ability to make things happen, or they can be given much narrower definitions. If we acquiesce in the much narrower definition, by accepting for purpose of discussion someone else's definition of "power" as what Jesus rejected rather than what he exercised, that terminological acquiescence must never be taken for a substantial concession. Jesus rejected the power of the

---

[12]66 Fordham Law Review 1089 (1998).

sword, of the lie, of social stratification...but he exercised other kinds of power effectively: the power of the truth, of love, of community....

My describing Jesus as "political," over against [Reinhold] Niebuhr's calling him "apolitical" [in The Politics of Jesus] made this same point. To set up the questions in such a way that to exist, to decide, and to act as a human-in-society is by definition to be culpable, as Niebuhr does, is to have denied the incarnation (to speak in dogmatic terms). The sinlessness of Jesus is not a merely dogmatic slogan. It is a statement about the possibility of authentic loving existence fully within the limits of humanity. But the point need not be made dogmatically; it can be made linguistically. To use "power" to describe what Jesus did is more whole, more "ordinary discourse" than to let Niebuhr say the capacity to defame or to kill is more basic. Niebuhr sets up the question that way, so that there can be no right action, by making "power" univocal, and yet at the same time saying that the power of the sword is at the center of the definition. (Feb. 22, 1989)

The Moral Force of Pacificism

In his book Nevertheless: The Varieties of Religious Pacifism (1977), John argued that lethal state violence is more naive than political pacifism:

"A society which hates its enemies and, although it says killing is wrong, punishes killers by killing them--thereby telling them that they were right (to kill)--is so twisted that it is unworthy of defense...." Utopian pacifism makes less of a leap of faith, he wrote, "than does the rhetoric which tells us that by forcibly making refugees, we are defending self-determination, or that by supporting a puppet government, we are enabling democracy to grow. There is no more utopian institution than an idealistic war." (p. 76)

"The only alternative to a cultic moralism which references life seems to be the equally cultic, arbitrary, unaccountable, and ungeneralizable obligations of patriotism." (p. 98)

"(A)ny known militarism in the real world shares all the vices of non-Christian pacifism. Militarism as well as pacifism is humanistic and utopian. It places enormous trust in the wisdom of administrative bureaucracy, in the moral insight of persons who have been hardened to think of other men as worthy of extermination." (p. 113)

In a review of Rene Girard's The Scapegoat, in Religion and Literature, in 1987, John wrote of the Crucifixion: "By assuming the status of innocent victim, Jesus destroyed the credibility of the persecuting majority's self-serving account, according to which the primal murder, at the foundation of all social order, was somehow just. The words of Caiaphas, 'It is expedient that one should die for the people,' and those of Jesus, 'They know not what they do,' can be taken straight. Jesus is revelatory in that he obliges violence to tip its hand, to reveal the fictitiousness of its self-justification." (p. 90)]

John supported the application of one of his undergraduate students, who sought to resign from the University's Air Force R.O.T.C. unit, on the grounds of conscientious objection. John wrote a memorandum on his undergraduate course; it apparently accompanied the application; John sent me a copy:

The course is a survey along historical lines, covering all of the different perspectives on the moral evaluation of war, including the "holy war" perspectives of ancient Israel and the Christian Crusades, all the way to modern "realism," including the pacifist minorities and the official "just war" teachings of the majority Christian tradition. By the nature of the case, it is the majority, "just war" perspectives which receive the fullest treatment. The course objective is to assist every student to make her or his moral decisions on a higher level of information than before; it excludes indoctrination.

[The cadet] was very independent in making his way through the study material, coming gradually to be more clear about the position which now has motivated him to take the unpopular stance we are now dealing with. As far as I am informed I can vouch for the sincerity and the self-motivated solidity of that moral and intellectual development.

I am most grateful for the ways in which the administration of the military services in the U.S.A. has institutionalized the country's respect for the freedom of conscience of men and women in the ranks, especially when they are persons whose age and assignments are such as to maximize growth and change. I am confident that [the student's] application will be processed correctly. (Feb. 2, 1996)

The application was referred to a legal officer, at an Air Force base in Ohio. That officer, by letter, requested from John a copy of the course syllabus used for the undergraduate theology course the cadet had taken from Yoder, and a list of reference materials used in the course, so that, he said, the Air Force lawyers could compare the reference material cited by the student with the course material used in the class. Yoder then sent the correspondence to me and asked for advice. Yoder to Shaffer:

Why should the credibility of [the cadet's] case be either stronger or weaker if it should be known that there was or was not some overlap between his studies in a required course in a Catholic university and his personal moral choices? ... If it should be confirmed that the reference material cited by [the cadet] in his application is or is not correlated with the course material, would that imply that [the Air Force] should have freedom to assign itself a supervisory role with regard to university instruction? [Should] either the university counsel or A.A.U.P. [American Association of University Professors, watchdog of academic freedom] be alerted? I have nothing to fear but maybe it should be an issue for the sake of the principle. Would it be appropriate for me, rather than simply sending off the syllabus to ask [the commander] some of these questions? (Feb. 14, 1996) [I recommended that John talk to the legal officer, who had offered his telephone number, and guessed that the officer's inquiry was more bureaucratic than anything else. John did not tell me anything further about what he did in the case. Maybe it is an interesting little example of how a county seat Hoosier lawyer sometimes helps keep the peace.

When the bishop says nuclear war is wrong and the laity go on fighting, you say the laity are not "taking seriously" the recent teaching of "their churches." But the laity are the church, too. Is the hierarchy's loss of credibility the fault of the laity? I agree that the bishops are reading the Just War Tradition more accurately than ever before, so that they have <u>a priori</u> a moral edge. But it is not liberal pluralism in the American polity which makes the laity ignore them. Nor is the Just War Tradition the Gospel of Jesus; it is itself a politically motivated dilution of the politics of Jesus, in the hope that people would listen better to a call to limit violence than to a call to abandon it. Paul in Romans 13 did want rulers to act, to reward the innocent and repress evil. Nero wasn't doing that, but Paul didn't doubt that that was his role. (Dec. 9, 1993)

Selective Conscientious Objection

Professor M. Cathleen Kaveny, a lawyer and law teacher as well as a theologian, John, and some other teachers got into a lunch-table discussion, in March, 1996, on two sub-categories of just-war doctrine. John had dealt with them in his <u>When War Is Unjust</u> (2d. ed. 1996), but he was, at the table that day, apparently listening. John often did that, at Notre Dame and in meetings I shared with him at gatherings of the Society of Christian Ethics. In this case, "selective" objection–meaning the conscription-eligible person's position of objection to some, but not all wars–is routinely associated with Roman Catholics and routinely not associated with members of "peace churches," such as John's. I found a copy of a memo John wrote to our colleague Kaveny in John's files.

Thank you for provoking and withstanding the response of several people at our table yesterday noon. I take advantage of the exchange to sort out some questions, without knowing where/whether/how I might make any further use of these observations. I did not join the table debate since I am less clear on these matters than some of your other interlocutors were, but I would like to pursue them in a more leisurely way....

I take it that you considered the case for "selective objection"...to be morally arguable and therefore legally worthy of a day in court when the refusal to obey is based on the killing of innocents, <u>i.e.</u>, a crime against "discrimination," since that evaluation is based on data which the individual soldier (deciding

whether to obey) or the individual citizen (deciding whether to accept being drafted) has access to.

On the other hand, you were challenging the ability of the individual to make such a judgment, and therefore the standing of his argument in court, when the evaluation was based on "proportion," because the empirical data on which such a judgment would have to be based are not public knowledge and the authorities know better.

I can agree that "discrimination" and "proportion" can be distinguished, although I have long been arguing that there are three interlocking concerns, not two.[13] Innocent immunity is the moral and legal principle. Discrimination is the capacity prerequisite to the ability to respect immunity. In Vatican usage, the two terms are telescoped, but the concepts are on different levels. If you cannot discriminate, i.e., if you cannot aim your weapons, then you can respect neither immunity nor proportion.

But, although the concepts are distinguishable, you lose me when you seem to be confident that in most settings, or in prototypical settings, one of these criteria clearly applies and the other not. My impression is that in most real cases both are in jeopardy. Not only is that the case in most real wars; it is also the case that most real, conscientious human beings are holistic, with many interlocking dimensions contributing to their moral positions.

Perhaps a larger question, for Vietnam at least, is the relevance of many other relevant criteria.... JWT [just war theory] is a complex of ten to twenty criteria, depending on how you count. Why pick on just those two and the logical difference between them when there are many others, most of them public and adjudicable with public criteria?

Back to your central theme: I can entertain hypothetically the notion that some of the data needed for a proportionality judgment would not be publicly accessible. But in real worlds that claim is outweighed by the demonstration (a) that those who do know things of that kind lie to us and even to themselves (Johnson, McNamara, Nixon) about those facts. They do not let those facts speak. (b) There are also other privilege knowers (like the Iraqi Roman Catholic community and the Pope in the case of the Gulf). (c) The burden of the proof is with the affirmative; if the advocates of a war cannot present their case in public data, that war cannot be justified. Even if the case "could probably" be made in the sense that the kinds of considerations which could be argued might exist, it is not a

---

[13] Both are sub-topics in just-war theory, both under the part of it that deals with the conduct of war (jus in bello). These terms are discussed in James F. Childress's short essays in his and John Macquarrie's Westminster Dictionary of Christian Ethics (1986) at pages 159 and 512.

moral case in public polity if the data claims cannot be demonstrated. When Richard Nixon said he had a secret plan for ending the war, that was a lie; it cannot serve as grounds <u>at the same time</u> (a) for keeping secret the data on which it is based <u>and</u> (b) for telling young draftees that what he is drafting them to do will be proportionate.

The court may have a moral right to ask that the CO exposit his reasons, especially if he claims to be a Catholic rather than a Quaker or Amish; but beyond ascertaining <u>that</u> he has reasons and <u>that</u> they are reasons of the kind that should count, it is not the court's business to evaluate whether he is using those reasons rightly. So to say that the judgment of the President or that of the Pentagon trumps the simple citizen would deny the whole notion of freedom of conscience. (Yoder to Kaveny, March 27, 1996)

In an appendix to <u>When War Is Just: Being Honest in Just War Thinking</u> (2nd ed. 1996), John outlined the two criteria under discussion in his letter to Professor Kaveny:

> VII. Means must be proportional.
>> A. The damage must not be greater than the damage prevented or the offense being avenged.
>> B. The damage or punishment inflicted must not be disproportionate to the guilt of the offender....
>> C. Proportion must be tested on every level.... A measure that appears disproportionate on one level may appear proportionate on a higher one.... The modest cost of a battle, on the other hand, may be wrong if the war is already lost....

IX. The means used must be discriminating, that is, subjected to measured control.

> This is prerequisite if proportionality (VII) and noncombatant immunity (VIII) are to be respected. If any weapon, any strategy, any military unit becomes uncontrollable, then that abandonment of discrimination infringes in principle upon the discipline of necessary and legitimate means.... If any government of command center <u>says</u> it intends to strike indiscriminately, that is already immoral as intention even though it has not been carried out.

On the Distinction Between Being a Scholar and Being a Pastor

John wrote, in a short memo to me, August 20, 1990, "...the distinctiveness of my orientation is not always that it answers differently a question which is already being asked so much as that it draws attention to other questions." And in notes in his file on Bob Rodes's theory of pluralism, he wrote, **"I'm not ready-- can't be neutral about overall society--clear manifestation of Chr. conscience can still be significant--can hold office."** He did not see his talents, though, as pastoral counseling talents. When Notre Dame teachers from a range of disciplines set out to assist Notre Dame R.O.T.C. students in facing questions on the Gulf War, he volunteered to be a resource, and to be politically active, but not to be a counselor. I found the following copy in John's files:

[With regard to] re-instating a counseling resource for students with regard to personal decisions derived from the teachings of the churches on war and peace...I do not think that what I am qualified for is what most of the counselees will need. I am however glad to be on call for anything which might involve a greater level of historical depth or complexity, whether in looking into the history of Christian thought or the testimony of the non-Catholic traditions." (Yoder to Father Richard V. Warner, C.S.C., December 13, 1990)

The component of my concerns...is the theme I have been pursuing ever since writing in 1955 the text which appeared in 1964 as <u>The Christian Witness to the State</u>. That is that I am not only against being drafted to kill people and against government when it is defined as oppression or what Michael Sattler called "the sword." I am also in favor of authentic servanthood in the public realm beyond the limits of the believing community. In rare situations like that of William Penn that can mean creative participation in the life of the civil order. It is epistemologically backward to put the question thus: "The state is defined as xxxx: Can the Christian have to do with it?" Proper epistemology would say: "The Kingdom of God is like....; what does that tell me to share with my neighbor, who has not joined me in following Jesus but whose human dignity I am pledged to affirm, in our common life?" Often there will be things to do that are of higher priority for the disciple to do than running the jails; but if so the reason for that is the stewardship of creativity, not a legalism which writes off certain territories. (September 20, 1991)

C. CAPITAL PUNISHMENT

The coercive power of the state is, I have found, an emotional presence among young people approaching the profession of law--a force they perceive as pressing on them more consciously after they have let law into their lives than before. I suppose this presence is different among young people approaching the profession of ministry and (not the same thing) the academic profession of theology, where it is perhaps less pressing and more insidious. Walter Brueggemann noted that "theology has not done very well at taking into account the reality of power." But these professions are practiced in the shadow of "the powers and dominions" as much as law is. John worked with one of these groups of young people; I work with the other.

With my population of students, the traditional tendency in America has been to attempt to make the emotional presence align with the claim, "Ours is a government of laws and not of men," which has tended in America to announce the presence of a god. A modern iconoclastic tendency among those who teach these young lawyers is to deny the claim, diminish the idolatry, and treat law as (mere) politics, or as the exercise of economic power--the "Crits" in one way of looking at things, the "law and economics movement" in another. I sought John's help in trying to stake out a position that would be theological, an appeal Yoder often thought naive. From what he and Stanley Hauerwas taught me, I came to appeal, often, to the Radical Reformation, which made it urgent to address the (as I think) undeniable awe a lawyer has for the law--whether "law" is taken in traditional piety or in modern disdain.[14] I sometimes tried to do this by putting lawyers in the church, as if they could be lawyers who look at the law from across the street from the courthouse. John repeatedly helped me with this, but hardly ever endorsed the way I was trying to do it:

I was not clear about how you made the move from the ecclesiological definition (people of God in the world of law) to the ethical specification (powerlessness...liberation). Is that ethical specimen one among many, so that parallel to it or instead of it, as defining the ethics of the people of God in the world of law, you could have put other ones (no lying, no theft, no adultery, no insulting father or mother, no blasphemy). Or is it in some sense deeper?

Do you mean it to strike at, to judge or to redeem sui generis the quintessence of the world of law as such, as those others would not? Do you suggest that the world of the lawyer deals with "power" as the banker, the factoryman, the farmer or the teacher or the soldier do not? It may be correct; if so, then to specify the special sense in which "power" is used there calls for more careful articulation....

You could do more...spelling out the...kinds of "power" or "force" that are not destructive. The liberation hermeneutic of [Gustavo] Gutierrez and [Robert E.] Rodes[15] is a part of it, but since liberation is defined negatively by contrast with

---

[14] I trace this a bit, in John's presence, in the short talk that became "How I Changed My Mind," 10 The Journal of Law and Religion 291 (1993-1994).

[15] John was probably thinking of Father Gutierrez's A Theology of Liberation (1968). Bob Rodes's "liberation hermeneutic" also cites that early and influential volume. (Gutierrez has written several others.) Rodes has developed his own way of reconciling the radicalism of Latin American liberation theology with

oppression, there are affirmative elements of Shalom which it may not identify. (Feb. 22, 1989)

*Entering the Capital-Punishment Debate,
In Court and Out*

[W]e must accept the facticity of the punitive drives, which will not go away simply by virtue of decent people's being ashamed of them. I suggest that such acceptance might illuminate the bad record of the U.S. with legal capital punishment. By telling the punishers they are bad people, maneuvering around them for a generation in the courts (shrewd lawyers badgering the prosecutors), the liberals only raised a new crop of more self-righteous punishers and a new crop of more refined punitive laws.

I would rather try, nonviolently accepting the punishers' inherited control of the cultural terrain, going the second mile to meet them, to grant that punishing has its place, and then to relativize it in various ways:

--by discerning many roots and functions for the punitive drive, rather than only one;

--by finding less lethal ways to satisfy the need; this includes, of course, the way the Oral Torah worked on the Mosaic rules...and the way the [local] Victim-Offender Reconciliation Program works in county courts, and the interventions in sentencing which Catholic law schools could be developing if they really bought the "seamless robe" or "consistent ethic" position....;

--by loving my own prosecutors, which is easier to do if I grant that there are reasons for their behaving like Bacchae....

I am working to spell out in detail how my accepting the rhetoric of punishment, which already dominates the world, although it is (in one sense, for those who know of Christ's victory) not legitimate, is more cognate to the way Jesus worked than it would be simply and by decree to declare the structures of the fallen world "illegitimate" or intrinsically impenetrable, like major atmospheric turbulence. [I had said that, to a Christian lawyer, the law was like the weather.] Actually, there are better and worse ways to survive and help the victims of storms, if one studies storm behavior, rather than ruling them out of the game, as did the

---

his natural-law jurisprudence, most notably in <u>Law and Liberation</u> (1986) and <u>Pilgrim Law</u> (1998). At about the time the latter volume was published, a group of Rodes's friends, John Howard Yoder among them, gathered at Notre Dame for a "conversation" about Rodes's Christian jurisprudence. The content was published in "The Christian Jurisprudence of Robert E. Rodes, Jr.," 73 <u>Notre Dame Law Review</u> 737 (1998), which I edited.

old, legal "act of God" language...

[T]his perspective would illuminate in a new way Paul's advice in I Cor. 6: "Why not accept mistreatment?" rather than always seeking justice. Being mistreated has a cultural function. Therefore accepting mistreatment has a cultural function. The fact that that fact runs counter to some other people's priority political agenda does not change its truth.

There is no ambivalence about the present stated position of the Roman Catholic bishops of this country on the death penalty. Since it was not always so, I suspect that (as is the case with Protestants) there are many of "the faithful" and maybe even some Catholic lawyers who do not share this view, but the episcopal documents are clear, and so are the opinions of those of your faculty with whom I have spoken, so I take the normative point as stipulated. (May 1993) [The question then would be what a Christian lawyer should do about capital punishment:]

John and I corresponded about my reluctance to enter, as a lawyer, into the last stages of a capital-punishment case--the sort of legal work the young lawyer did in John Grisham's novel The Chamber. I felt--and I am not sure John talked me out of feeling--that my probably vain efforts to frustrate the executioner with the law were more in aid of the system than in aid of changing it.

Obviously a lawyer is always helping the courts to operate. [Such a lawyer need] not propose to defend someone because that would mean collaborating in possibly killing them. There is something odd about thinking that a dissenter is morally responsible for the evil which he objects to just because he accepts communicating his dissent in the setting where the evil is about to be done. (May 20, 1993)

One focus for trying to discuss law as power is law as lethal, legal power imposing death (war, capital punishment) or used to countenance the imposition of death (euthanasia, abortion). I had, for example, ventured the opinion, citing something John wrote, that the temporary success of efforts of anti-capital-punishment lawyers in the federal supreme court in 1972 had turned out to be "useless." John bridled at that word, and explained his disagreement in a way that illustrates his consistent ethical teaching that witness is not measured by effectiveness:

One of the fascinating ways in which you provoke learning is that you feed back pictures of myself which I do not recognize. I do not think that the victory of the ACLU or the Legal Defense Fund which led to the provisional suspension of capital punishment in 1972 was useless. Since I believe in trying to follow a man who was ultimately defeated in terms of human social process, I have to be much more ambivalent about the meaning of words like "useless."

But I do not think I am alone in recognizing that after having won many small skirmishes and several apparently decisive battles, the good guys in this struggle lost the war. And in contrast with the rest of the civilized world, our

society from the grass roots up is moving toward more rather than less vindictive killing. I do not think that the reason the war was lost was that the battles were won. It was better to fight them than not, and it was better to win them when it could be done with the truth than to lose them. That does not change the nature of the vindictive reflex in our culture....

American Roman Catholics on Capital Punishment

Just recently...it occurred to me that there is an odd pun in the standard use of the word "faithful." In ordinary Catholic journalism and sociology, I think that the word means the laity as distinguished from the leadership. But when you undertake an opinion survey to know what "the faithful" think, especially since Cardinal Newman said they should be consulted as some kind of an inchoate theological resource, one discovers that on very important questions, of which capital punishment is one, the position they hold is opposite to the Gospel as interpreted both by the hierarchy and by me. So "the faithful" does not mean automatically people who are guided by what most of us consider "the faith." (May 20, 1993)

[There has been] a recent initiative by some people in Elkhart to join a nationwide publicity effort on the subject of the death penalty. I have never quite understood the combination of commitment and objectivity with which [the Notre Dame] campus deals with capital punishment as a legal institution. I know that your colleague Tex [Professor Fernand Dutile] has worked on the subject within the discipline academically, but I have no memory of ever having heard that it gets talked about in regular teaching, either in political science or in your school. If it does, knowing that would be something somebody in my department could reinforce and celebrate. (January 20, 1993)

[I had written in a draft that the Christian way to deal with Rambos is to endure them:] That should include naming them, denouncing them publicly, and organizing communal support for the victims, even celebrating the victims; to say "inventing new rules against Rambos" is not enough--is true but is not enough.... (December 29, 1992)

D. CIVIL DISOBEDIENCE

During March and April, 1991, John had a running correspondence on plans by the editor of the Notre Dame Journal of Law, Ethics, and Public Policy, Martin Loesch, to do a symposium issue on civil disobedience. John declined the opportunity to write an essay on the subject, but did, finally, agree to write the foreword to the symposium.

I was not able to respond with anything solid to the earlier invitation to prepare an article, because the concept of "civil disobedience" would seem in my mind to demand too much cross-cultural definition and refinement before it could have any relevance to the interpretation of the New Testament. (Yoder to Martin Loesch, February 6, 1991)

As it turned out, John's "Foreword" was perhaps the essay Mr. Loesch had in mind in the first place. Omitting the references, and some of the text, as well as John's description, toward the end of the foreword, of the symposium papers written by others, this is from the manuscript version I found in John's files; it is used here with the editors' permission:

By the nature of the case, the concept of civil disobedience cannot be self-defining. It designates a response to a particular demand of a particular governmental authority, because the person who would ordinarily be willingly subject to that authority holds its dictates to be overruled by a higher power. Both the unacceptable claim and the higher power are incorrigibly particular, unique.

In principle the case for disobedience is classically simple; if there be a God worthy of the name, then that God's claims, when known, must by definition be imperative. The only honor that God's servants owe to anyone else is what is compatible with the prior divine will. Formally speaking, the only exception to this logic would be a situation where a given state would itself be divinely mandated. This was thought to obtain in ancient Mesopotamia and ancient Egypt. It could obtain in some readings of Constantine's divine mandate, yet only because the God in question was no longer JHWH of hosts, the Father of Jesus. In principle, no state today being God, when seen from the perspective of those who believe, the notion of a case where "we must obey God rather than men" must not be impossible.

On the other hand, any state considers itself in some sense to be a moral absolute, a "sovereign"; it cannot by definition be prevented from making some claims which some of its subjects consider improper. Even those modern western states which limit themselves by means of written or implicit Bills of Rights do so sovereignly.

What remains open for definition in particular cases, then, is the grounds for identifying some particular demand of the state as unacceptable to some citizen. When that happens, the second question is whether, and if so how, the state will (or "can afford to") accede to such a refusal.

Prototype: The Pagan Cult

The simplest classical specimen is obligatory participation in a pagan cult, dramatized in the heroic legend of Daniel:

> Your question hardly requires an answer; if
> our God, the one we serve, is able to save us

> from the burning fiery furnace and from your
> power, O king, he will save us; and even if he
> does not, then you must know, O king, that we
> will not serve your god or worship the statue
> you have erected.

But the cult example may overstate the issue, as if the only ground for disobedience were formal idolatry. Those same four friends had been just as stubborn two chapters earlier in defense of their Jewish dietary commitment. Yet one trait in the picture which we may carry over from the ancient examples is the awareness that the line which limits obedience is easier to draw for persons who have a strong realistic sense of cult meanings; we think of the meanings of blood or of the flag for Jehovah's Witnesses.

It is a different matter when in a relativistic and nominalistic culture one asks where the limits of compliance run....

There are at least two classical ways to define a point of imperative resistance. One was articulated by Martin Luther King, Jr., in his classic <u>Letter from Birmingham City Jail</u>:

"[T]here are two types of laws: just and unjust. I would be the first to advocate obeying just laws.... [O]ne has a moral responsibility to disobey unjust laws...."

If we set aside for the moment the question of how one knows that a given law is immoral, this argument can serve to restate the point of mandatory resistance.... He is writing to religious leaders and making a religious claim. But how is that "non-law," which ought not to be obeyed, identified as such?.... [Dr. King:] "An unjust law is a code that is out of harmony with the moral law. To put it in the terms of St. Thomas Aquinas: An unjust law is a human law that is not rooted in eternal law and natural law...." The concept is very clear, but few of our readers will take that definition as adequate to guide legislation or litigation.

The other classical conceptual weapon to limit obedience is the notion of an intrinsically evil deed. It occurs at numerous points in routine Catholic moral theology. In his article on "War" in the <u>Catholic Encyclopedia</u> (1912), Charles Macksey, then Professor of Ethics and Natural Rights at the Gregorian University, included within the criteria for means within the "just war" that there be <u>no act intrinsically immoral</u>. It is assumed that there exist (or may exist) such acts; that they can be identified; and that once identified they both should and can be refused....

Most of the above survey of simple types of argument has centered on the burden of proof's being with the negative; why and when must one <u>not</u> obey? A.J. Muste reverses the burden of proof, in an evangelical way consonant with the doctrine of vocation taught by his Calvinist ancestors. The Christian (or any decent person) is (or should be) already doing what God has called him or her to do. It is not for the state to oblige any subject by force to leave that calling even if the thing the state wants her or him to do were not evil. Even if the government offers noncombatant alternative service to the pacifist, its right to call the citizen away from her or his primary calling must be contested. This may sound to some like anarchism or libertarianism; it is, rather, Puritan.

The Tactical Dimension

Thus far I have been reviewing the **prima facie** argument for not obeying. It applies to Jehovah's Witnesses refusing transfusions, or to the early Christian martyrs; yet there is a quite different dimension in most of the important stories. Neither Gandhi nor King disobeyed **every** unjust law. Which law to break and why (and when) was determined in the light of shrewd strategic thinking, with a view to changing the unjust laws by unmasking their injustice in the eyes of the wider public, or of the people benefitting from their enforcement. Thus what at first looked like a firm deontological "So help me God I cannot do otherwise" is at the same time a carefully calculated pragmatic tool for achieving change which one could not attain by the ballot or the gun. The deontological appeal is the stated grounds for breaking the law; but the pragmatic intent is what builds a constituency. The deontological appeal is why the position is called "conscientious" and why governments concede exemptions, but standing alone it can be accused of purist irresponsibility. The pragmatic intent claims relevance but at the cost of debatable tactical calculations about effectiveness.

The trick is to keep both dimensions decisive without collapsing either into the other. Without the pragmatic promise, the "Here I Stand" rhetoric is overblown, discrediting its own transcendent claim. Without the transcendent claim, the pragmatism boils down to mere obstructionism grasping for illegitimate leverage in the service of a minority interest. Thus each dimension must be evaluated in its own terms: the transcendent by the criteria of moral discourse and the pragmatic as social strategy. The debate is incorrigibly bifocal. We may think we differ about the social description when the clash is really between moral commitments, or vice versa.

This review of the ordinary resources for limiting obligation to government must suffice to have located the concept we are pursuing. If the state is not god its claims must be finite. The concept of "limit" is operational only if in some real case a greater value can in fact claim priority; then the moral thing to do is to disobey. If there is no place for this to occur, the state is god after all. Yet if it is done routinely it undermines the more normal vehicles of political discourse.

Chapter Three

Ethics and Eschatology

A. ESCHATOLOGY

I borrow for the title of this chapter the title of the paper John wrote for what his file notes as the "North Park Symposium," in October, 1990, and which was quoted at the beginning of the last chapter. The following excerpts from that paper establish a point of view that, in my opinion, can characterize John's ethic, as the excerpts in the last chapter described his jurisprudence: While his ethic was remarkably eclectic and open, although, as the theologians say, also radically "Christocentric," it was, as I learned it, recurrently eschatological. Those four words point to the substance of this chapter and the substance of Yoder's theological ethic: (i) eclectic: He was the least doctrinaire ethicist I have read–and, as Hoosier lawyers go, I have read a lot of them; (ii) open: What distinguished John among thinkers in the "free church" tradition was his consistent willingness to listen to other ethics scholars, his acceptance of their language of argument, and his generous interest in ethical traditions other than his own; (iii) Christocentric: "Jesus is Lord" was fundamental in John's moral reasoning; that, more than a more traditional stance within Protestant history, explains the jurisprudence of the last chapter, as it also explains the ethics of this chapter; and (iv) eschatological–as you will now see:

"Ethics" is not an independent mode of access to the understanding of either ancient documents or ancient ideas; it is rather one subdiscipline of theology. It has to be constructed on the foundations laid by the community's history. In the mix of the disciplines it needs to listen to those other specialists who read in their settings....

To discern what apocalypse does for ethics--perhaps also with regard to worship, or ecclesiology, or soteriology, but at least with regard to ethics–we need therefore to center our attention not on the immediate sense of distance with which particular assumptions of moral relevance strike us, as for instance the rewarding of continence in John's Chapter 14 or the judgment on merchants in Chapter 18. We should ask rather about the overall cosmological and eschatological frame of reference within which value judgments occur.... I speak here of ethics as the architectonics of moral choice, concerned less with what we should decide and do than with how we think about deciding and doing. I should attend more to dissimilarity than to resonance; more to what is hard for us moderns to appropriate empathetically than to what seems self-evidently clear to us.

Many of the subdisciplines which aid us in interpreting the scriptures may, when taken in isolation, fall short of aiding the texts to discharge that function. One instance, which enormously preoccupied generations of scholars, especially Protestants, was the debate of high scholasticism about the unique epistemological status of "Scripture" as a kind of proposition different from other propositions because of their having been written uniquely under "inspiration." From this were derived further fruitless debates about "inerrancy," or [about] "infallibility," just as fruitless....

For the consequentialism which justifies the compromises of powerful people to make sense, one must assume a fully known causal nexus; otherwise one cannot argue to justify this or that sacrifice of one value for another, the breaking of this rule for the sake of that objective. The structural pastoral attention to the pros and cons of particular decisions, which in the age of Pascal gave to Jesuits and to "casuistry" a bad name, began with the assumption that there was a closed system with only two choices, each costly, neither one compatible with all of one's moral imperatives. The quandary became the paradigm for moral discourse. Hard cases on the edge of ordinary experience became the way to test the reach of one's principles. <u>Exceptio probat</u>, the exception tests the rule....

I attend here to the axiom of the closed moral nexus, with two and only two choices, both of them bad. This assumes the closed world view from which the seers' vision not only of divine agency but even of human agency calls us to be freed.[16] There are other choices, some foreseeable and others not. If we call those other possibilities "miracle," our contemporaries will sneer; but we can also call them creativity or surprise. The closed nexus breaks down as soon as there are more parties to the process, each with some degree of unpredictability if not freedom.

I am not sure what value to give another kind of argument which some

---

[16]The "North Park" excerpt in the last chapter locates the term "seer."

thinkers in the realm of science and religion take quite seriously, namely the way in which the natural sciences today are painting a less orderly, less machine-like picture of things, with Heisenbergian uncertainty about measuring subatomic particles, or with turbulence in fluid systems, or with fits and starts in species evolution. I am not sure that such loosening of the mechanistic vision by the natural scientists makes room for human or even divine freedom, but it certainly is compatible with our refusing to let a hopeless dilemma be the last word. If the cosmos is not closed, then what seemed <u>prima facie</u> to be the lesser evil may well not be the least evil.

Retrieving an Apocalyptic Style

There is yet another way in which contemporary thought is retrieving, not always very carefully, an apocalyptic style. Human intervention can so interfere with the ecosphere as to make the world uninhabitable. Jonathan Schell's <u>The Fate of the Earth</u> predicted that history as we know it would be ended by a nuclear exchange; others had said it of the way the arms race had changed the world, even without war. Others have discerned the "end of history as we now know it" in the collapse of the Soviet Empire, or in the end of the ability of ideologies to convince, or in the overloading of the ecosphere. Ethical sobriety demands that we take all of these new thresholds seriously; but is that eschatology?

The notion that system-immanent thought has declared itself at an end has itself become not only thinkable but trendy. It is not in this sense that I would advocate a retrieval of the seers' freedom from claimed "realism." The seers differ from this recent trend in that they proclaim the "known world" to be too small, not because they have from the inside come to the edge of it, but because God has reached and spoken into it from beyond. In our age "transcendence" is sometimes a code word for the fact that, from within our own system, we know ourselves to be finite, thereby creating by extrapolation the notion of "beyond" even though there be nothing (nothing we can know) "out there." Prophetic transcendence comes from the other end; the "beyond" came first. Divine command, divine agency, divine will are prior to, not derived from, extrapolated from our finitude. An ethic of <u>Torah</u> and <u>halakah</u>, or an ethic of discipleship, is therefore deeper, more rooted in the nature of things, than an ethic which seeks to manipulate the causal nexus for the best.

These are only sample soundings. My hope is that the oddity of the literature of the seers may continue to shake or to shock us into the recognition that the limits our moral systems impose on our moral possibilities need not be the last word.

Toward the end of his paper [in the North Park symposium] John J. Collins describes apocalypse as "a way of looking at the world which...cannot be

Ethics and Eschatology

verified factually but only authenticated in value by the kind of action it supports.... The ethical stance...gives rise to the eschatological vision just as much as it draws support from it." This points to a fruitful way of restating the question. To say simply that "apocalypse is validated by the ethics it sustains" would be a wrongly reductionist horizontalism. It would also be self-defeating, since the vision will only support the ethos if the seer considers God and revelation to be real. It would also be petitionary; by what standards from beyond the system would one validate the "kind of action it supports"? But to say that there is a spiral of complementarity, whereby the ethic supports the promise and vice versa, both of them contradicting both the fallen world's defeatism and the fallen Powers' oppression, may enable us to describe both as doxology. The adequacy of the seers' vision is rehearsed and celebrated not so much in the fulfilment of the events they predict as in the divine nature which the predictions clothe and in the liberated life of those who believe. [North Park, 1990]

Covenantal Sociality

Eschatology is the deeper and more important part of John's ethic. In another and earlier venue, though, he gave his subject a more exactly communal and scriptural focus. The following is part of his contribution to a panel discussion on New Testament ethics, in 1980, at a meeting of the American Academy of Religion. The paper is published in full in <u>To Hear the Word</u>:

"The genus <u>homo</u> is an ethicizing and meaning-mongering animal. Doing ethics is a fundamental trait of the race before there are words for it. To be human means to be human together. To be human together means to expect of one another behavior that will make sense (i.e. that will conform to certain patterns present in our memory and in our expectations before we talk about them). Those expected patterns, to which most people must conform most of the time if the genus is to survive, constitute the <u>ethos</u>. There may be some human society somewhere whose identity has no special component that could be identified as ethical, but there is no reason for that odd eventuality to interest us....

"It cannot be different in any subset of the genus. A constitutive element of participating authentically in the family <u>christianus</u> within the species <u>sapiens</u> of the genus <u>homo</u> is knowing how to behave, knowing why to behave thus, and developing tools of discourse to help one another thus to behave. This common sense background should not need to be said, yet its obviousness is sometimes forgotten. Moral obligation is not something added on to being human, or to being a believer, by some supplemental revelatory event; it is one dimension of what is already there. Therefore it is not merely difficult or debatable, but impossible to 'found' ethics somewhere outside of itself or outside of faith.

"The ethical dimension of being Christian is thus a constitutive element of covenantal sociality. It can be talked about in individual terms, but its shared quality is logically prior to when an individual becomes a Christian or when that individual talks about it. The ethicist is a servant of the communal identity, not its founder or its ruler.

"This community identity is not provincially particular. It is not separate from the rest of humanity, in the sense that it could not be transported, translated or projected into other cultures with other histories. Yet neither is it publicly generalizable. It cannot be imposed upon persons who do not share its axioms. It is understandable and usable only in the context of stated (or at least shared if unstated) assumptions and affirmations with regard to the sovereignty of God and the Lordship of Jesus Christ. It therefore refuses to subject itself to the rules of those for whom to be publicly accountable means to be generalizable." (pp. 107-108)

B. NATURAL LAW JURISPRUDENCE

I asked John's advice on an article I was asked to do for the Christian Legal Society Quarterly, on what the editor of that journal called "the ethics explosion"[17]:

I doubt very much that it would be either possible or desirable to have a single reading with regard to the society as a whole on such a broad question. Various sets of people would decry or welcome the waning of various kinds of moral codes.

Each kind of code and each kind of waning would call for an important ethical analysis but there is no reason to assume that they would be the same.

A large number of people think that the "good old days" have fallen apart because there does not exist a standard moral code which is acknowledged by all and supported by the state and reinforced by the police. But when there was such a position it was coercive, was not supported by the conviction of most of the people, and represented a Constantinian confusion of the faith community with the civil community.

So the falling away of some kinds of moral consensus is actually a clearing of the decks for a better way of understanding the rootage of morality in the will.

Certainly one of the reasons that when people are looking for ethics they do not look at the churches, is that the way in which the churches commended the ethical insights which they thought were right did not convince. Sometimes this was because the Christians themselves did not live according to the rules which

---

[17]It was in the Summer 1993 issue.

they wanted to enforce on other people. Other times the Christians would in fact argue that one does not need to be Christian in order to have those convictions (which is the tradition of the "natural law")–so obviously there is nothing lost by not consulting the churches.

In short: Don't quote me, but I have the impression that the question is so broad that there is hardly anything one can do about it without disentangling the several different levels of meaning and concern. (February 24, 1993)

"Sectarian" Ethics

I used John's thought on natural law in an article in <u>America</u>, roughly similar to what appears just above, not citing Yoder for it, though–citing two Roman Catholic theologians instead. This provoked a prompt letter to the editor from John's and my colleague, the late Father Richard McCormick, S.J., labeling that view of natural law as "sectarian."

I was thinking of writing earlier about your piece in <u>America</u> and Richard McCormick's answer to it.

It is good that you wrote to Dick that you found the question in Himes and Himes, but McCormick's reference to your sectarian friends is understandable, since in the place in your <u>America</u> paper to which he responded you had just attributed your [other] thoughts [on the theology of vocation] to me.

I often feel an inclination to object when you or Stanley [Hauerwas] attribute to me some insight which I am not sure I should claim paternity for. The "natural law" argument is several cans of worms; I would only speak of "natural law argumentation" in a particular instance because in each usage something else is at stake. The way your <u>America</u> passage characterized [implied at <u>most</u> that] <u>my</u> criticism was not false but was oversimple, thus making room for Dick's oversimple response. (January 6, 1997)

With a sense that four such theologians are looking over my shoulder as I look up and excerpt the relevant passages from my little essay in the Jesuit weekly, "The Christian Lawyer–An Oxymoron?" (a title appended by the editor), <u>America</u>, Nov. 23, 1996, p. 15:

If we lawyers were to turn to Christian theology–what Dietrich Bonhoeffer called "the memory of the church"–for help, we would notice at least three theoretical starting points: The theology of <u>vocation</u> would be one. <u>Natural law theory</u> would be the other. And what might be called the <u>sectarian</u> alternative would be a third. The first two, I will argue, won't help much. The sectarian approach will.

The Fathers of the Reformation, particularly Martin Luther, developed the theory that each of us, in her or his work in life, is called to serve the neighbor in a way that is both biblical and specifically vocational. Luther's doctrine went so far as to affirm a morality that is inherent in each vocation. That would call for a Christian lawyer to examine what she is up to, as a lawyer, and to discern the morality that is inherent in doing that thing.

Take, for example, the matter of a lawyer serving the guilty. The doctrine of vocation would be a Christian way to do what the American legal profession has done, to justify serving the system.....

I don't suppose this line of Christian thinking would lead inevitably to trusting the system to provide justice. Perhaps Luther would be the first to notice that if you push this thinking far enough, you trust the state more than faith allows. You trust the state, not only to be a source of justice, but to be right; [and] the state is often wrong. You could even begin to put the state where God ought to be; Martin Luther would not sit still for that. The Reformed Church tradition of John Calvin...–with its insistence that the world and all of its occupations are a theater for the glory of God, that every calling is a calling under God–would, I think, be wary of separating vocational morality [even as far] as Luther did.

The biblical and theological problem is that the Protestant doctrine of vocation, like Catholic natural law theory, separates ordinary Christians from the Christian who happens to be a specialist. It separates them socially, **as John Howard Yoder puts it, "so that what separates [Christians] from one another is held to be more important for their social behavior than what they have in common in Christ...."** When applied to Christian lawyers in modern America, the morality of vocation lets **"the most important specification of how persons should behave be one which separates them from brothers and sisters by saying that their calling under God is contradictory both to Christ's guidance and to what others should do."**

Yoder claims correctly that Catholic natural law thinking is "hardly structurally different." Like Luther's doctrine of vocation, natural law morality depends on perception and reason separated from the faith of the believing community.

Jurisprudence Is Ethics (Maybe)

I found in John's files handwritten notes he had made for a talk he gave to my law-school class in jurisprudence, on March 4, 1991. The students had read parts of Bob Rodes's The Legal Enterprise. Much of what John noted to say was to puzzle over whether jurisprudence is even a discipline (Rodes would say it is):

Separate discipline: "law" as if stable: different attitudes toward it. No help thus far. Looks like ethics--some Chr., some commonsensical. Critique not novel--basic Chr.--in fact basic Jewish. "Sectarian" only in sense of modern sociol. typology, E. Troeltsch. The elements of "Constantine" which matter to

critique are mostly in the Rodes text.

What does Constantine mean for ethics? Note in the outline: no ethics, no theology. Real Caesar a corrupt megalomaniac: pagan cult, military dictatorship, blood cult of gladiatorial entertainment. Constantine did not forsake this on "becoming a Christian"–"becoming" [had] no meaning for him--no change in ethics for him--change in worship and theology also went the other way.

Changes in the "ethic": (1) Constantine the elect divine instrument (Eusebius). (2) Constantine as representative failure.... Other source of moral guidance. (3) "Common sense" as consensus. (4) "Common sense" as skill. What if everybody....: (5) consequentialism, (6) generalizable a la Kant. Not a fair criticism. (7) Everyman, no motive, no commitment, no conversion. (8) Augustine; impossibility of the good. Not fact of falling short, but ontological. Last word. (March 4, 1991)

In connection with that jurisprudence class, and John's visit to it, I asked him to point to something I could give the students as preparatory reading:

I cannot think of anything that would be more representative than my 1964 pamphlet, which has been printed again, as The Christian Witness to the State. What I would do for the class would not be to digest it or interpret it or translate it into Catholic, but rather to indicate why the questions that matter to me are the questions which it approaches rather than someone else's questions about "what is law" or about "is law natural?" (Jan. 4, 1991)

[He had asked me, in the preceding August, to be cautious in telling the students what to expect:] I'm not sure the best way to describe my convictions is that they come from my denominational background. This leads people to project in inappropriate ways from their understanding of the Amish rejection of culture or the pacifist rejection of power. (August 24, 1990)

[On an undated piece of conference-center notepaper, headed "Ball Jurisprudence, Barth or Religion," John wrote:] Is [there] such a thing as "law"; describe attitudes of various people to it. (A) No such ONE thing--too many meanings. Saddam Hussein is law etc. (B) K. Barth; religion is not an univocal category, not all good. (C) Phenomenon of discussion claiming to be for good. Classical tradition assumes Good. Apoc. looks at case where not. (Undated)

I asked John to look at the draft of an essay called "The Tension Between Law in America and the Religious Tradition." He focused, in reply, on a comparison I made between the positions of Stanley Hauerwas and the Rev. Richard John Neuhaus, who was then a Lutheran pastor and who later became a Roman Catholic priest:

I am a little unsure about the statement...according to which the argument between Hauerwas and Neuhaus is an internal argument according to the rules of the believing community. It seems to me rather that it is partly an argument about whether it is appropriate that the believing community should be dominantly committed to internal integrity (Hauerwas) or whether the responsibility of that community to provide for the prosperity of the civil order should overrule the internal fidelity whose norm is Jesus.

Certainly Dick claims to be orthodoxly Lutheran on matters of dogma: but when he talks about the public square he is committed to be American, and to let even America be defined from the top down.... I think it is interesting to see what Dick would say about your putting him in the same category with Stanley and suggesting that both of them are carrying out a task which you credit me with describing. (April 1, 1987)

Showing What I Mean By "Eclectic" and "Open"

You comment that Tom Potter [a Massachusetts lawyer, Methodist minister and long-time leader in the <u>Journal of Law and Religion</u>] "relies on justice" more than you can see "working." I assume you mean "relies on the adequacy of the concept," i.e. that the reliance in question is epistemological rather than moral. Personally I don't think any concepts are reliable. The ways I have indirectly testified to my distrust of such language moves have been:

--questioning the self-evidence of the claims "liberation" theologians make for violence being justified by its claim to liberate;

--questioning the language game whereby "violence" is given different meanings, whereby the "structural" is the other guy's fault and is worse;

--questioning the usability of the notion of "nature" as in Catholic self-characterizations, whereby the term means both how things are and how they should be but are not.

One can say that each of these arguments is an angle on the notion that "justice" is independently knowable as a value. (October 23, 1993)

John put a particular meaning on the claim the church is universal. Based on a reflection both from Karl Barth and from the history of the Free Church, John said, a kind "of incipient universalism is that of the confessing minority whose commitment to her Lord, despite its being against the stream, is so convinced of the majesty of his Lordship that she risks trusting that his power and goodness can reach beyond the number of those who know him by his right name. The former universalism is a high view of the human; the latter a high view of Jesus." (Unpublished, an epilogue written after a lecture entitled "The Basis of Barth's Social Ethics," 1978, Karl Barth Society, Elmhurst, Illinois.)

Ethics and Eschatology

Is Bob [Rodes's] criterion of "transcendence of the human person"[18] an adequate surrogate for all the dimensions of the difference faith makes? Or is it the core of a much larger skein of indispensable functional traits? If [administrators of the University of Notre Dame] used that as criterion would "the Catholic character" of Notre Dame be safe? ...

Whether the American intellectual "common core" is described out of Tocqueville and Judge Holmes, or out of Grotius, I need more help to see how Bob's saying "the common core is too attenuated" and "we must reach across differences" (as an empirical reading of the present pluralistic scene) connects with the classical "Natural Law" claims that are supposed to be valid for everyone and not dependent on what other people believe. To say that Grotius "sought out and articulated common ground" looks to me like a positivist reconstrual of what Grotius did. Grotius thought he was in the classical tradition in which the laws of nations and of nature coincided from way back when. Where we think the common value core came from makes a difference for what rhetoric we will use to respond when the "common core" gets thinner. Bob's suggestion of backing into standing alone when the common core gets too thin looks to me like the Constantinian caricature of the motivation of the Radical Reformation....

You say you don't know about analogies in Rabbinic Judaism. The categories have to shift. The Rabbis from the fall of Jerusalem until the development of Western tolerant states were lawyers. Of course, they were scripture scholars; that is what lawyers do. They were more like lawyers than like priests or counselors or mystics. (April 26, 1994)

Communal Discernment

John had warned, in his essay "The Hermeneutics of Peoplehood," first published in the <u>Journal of Religious Ethics</u> (1982) and then as a chapter in <u>The Priestly Kingdom</u>, against letting this search for what he called "the search for a public moral language" be "motivated...by embarrassment about particularity...not willing to break through...to confession."

In his critique of H. Richard Niebuhr's <u>Christ and Culture</u>, he wrote: "Those who seek to modify society by taking a 'more positive attitude' toward it are actually rendered unable to do so, when by 'positive attitude' they mean abandoning an independent standpoint."

---

[18]In <u>Pilgrim Law</u>, I suspect, perhaps in explication of the Vatican II document <u>Gaudium et Spes</u>. References in the next paragraph are to Rodes's essay in Father Hesburgh's book; this essay is discussed here in Chapter One.

Moral Memoranda From John Howard Yoder

"The consistency which counts," he wrote there, "is the concrete community process of discernment, as that community converses, in the light of the confession 'Christ is Lord,' about particular hard choices.... It is the actual functioning fellowship of the church within human experience which validates claims to have known the will of God.... 'Transformation' is meaningful and accountable only when those who call for it have a place to stand." (p. 74) This was by way of stating disagreement with both the Lutheran doctrine of vocation and traditional Roman Catholic natural-law theory--in both cases because these points of view accord to "culture" "stability it does not have.... (A)ll such structures are in flux." (p. 78)]

Julia Meister and I wrote an article in the Duke Law Journal (1997), complaining about the way "appropriate" and "inappropriate" are used as weasel words for announcing moral judgments. With John's help, and that of Stanley Hauerwas, we were able to move from that negative position to suggest for lawyers and judges an ethic and jurisprudence rooted in communal perceptions of what is fitting.

You are quite right to want to make something of the way in which judgments of "appropriateness" make moral assumptions and claims.... By the nature of the case, as a subset of the "nature" epistemology, most of the people who make those assumptions/arguments assume self-evidence and therefore do not present warrants.

The one analog in my memory is that Max Stackhouse did a survey (or had his assistants do so) of the contents of a large number of texts on professional ethics. Many of them used the notion of "fittingness" in the way you are interested in, which meant clothing a normative claim in the form of a descriptive one. At that time I saw it as one more run on the Christ/Culture grid from H Richard....

Stackhouse's tacit thesis was that the way people structure the outline of a textbook is already revelatory, showing you the shape of the discipline, which is therefore automatically something to "fit" into. That there might be right action which would not "fit" the setting, or that there might be important data that would not "fit" the outline (two different forms of unfittingness) are notions the system cannot deal with.... (August 15, 1995)

When Catholics Say "Naturally"

I have been here for almost thirty years now trying to understand what Catholics mean when they say "naturally!" It is basically the same as when a Jewish mother says "because!" It means, "I have already defined the terms of the debate." It is not a clear epistemology about how to define and validate concepts. It is a power statement about who defines the community. (January 6, 1997)

Ethics and Eschatology

The Insanity Defense

Rationale for killing, and the insanity defense. As people like Kaczynski [the accused "Unabomber"] keep the variations on the insanity defense on our minds, I find myself remembering your citing Justice Holmes to the effect that a dog knows the difference between being kicked on purpose and being stumbled over unintentionally.

    (a)   **Not having observed many dogs being kicked, I am not sure this is true.**

    (b)   **If it is true, I am not sure that a court deciding whether to kill a killer either is or should be analogous to a dog deciding whether to bite my ankle.**

Insanity, whether like M'Naughton not knowing the difference between good and evil or like the Unabomber being paranoid and schizoid, is not a matter of inattentiveness like stumbling. A dog could say that people who stumble should also have their ankles bitten, so that they learn to watch where they are going. The malice of the kicker is not the dog's only reason for biting back. (Dec. 30, 1997, the day John Howard Yoder died)

Politics

[Notes in a file John marked "Shaffer/Rights"; from 1988:] A legal argument is invitation to a moral world.... Trouble assuming Dr. in bioeth. as <u>friend</u>; is rather mechanic.... To be open in friendliness to all, requires charity as infused virtue.... To be human is to be political. To renounce violence is not to be apolitical. Resort to violence is a breakdown of polis, not its definition.... Cath. vision optimistic human nature...Prot./Anglican basically suspicious.... Can't come from reason [or] nature.

C. ON USING STORIES IN CHRISTIAN ETHICS

John had persistent difficulty with the use of "narrative" as a starting place for arguments in theological ethics--the penchant of Stanley Hauerwas and, to some extent, Alasdair MacIntyre, both of whom were colleagues of ours at Notre Dame--and, in legal ethics, a derivative penchant of my own[19]:

I am sorry to be a burden by asking, again, when it arises from the conversation: What makes a story good, or a person good?--the question which you

---

[19] I tried to defend my penchant to my law-teacher audience in a review published at 33 <u>American Journal of Jurisprudence</u> 241 (1988).

say bothers you as you drive around.... My point is not that stories do not have moral meaning...nor that "a good person" is not meaningful language (which you seem to think I am doubting, when you appeal to Aristotle).

What I ask about is the criteria for what is a good man, or what is a good story, or how, when you think you have a good story, you can convince me it is a good story, or how you think a story conveys meaning. Being biblical, one can say that to answer that criteriology question it is proper to appeal, beyond the fictional lawyer stories you read, to the (true) macrostory of Abraham, Moses, Jeremiah, Jesus.... That is what I suggested...would make sense. But even with the privileged macro story, the scribes and prophets do not make the claim that good stories, biblical or otherwise, exegete themselves univocally. You seem to me to be tacitly making that claim, but you only make it tacitly, because to make it overtly would be contradictory. Yet when you make it only tacitly, you can't understand the questions I ask on that level.

In real life there are notions already built into the culture; there are vents; there are institutions; there are persons; there are the factual data of the material world, each of these dimensions being meaningful, in terms of the others. Reality is multidimensional, just as is the hermeneutics of peoplehood. [Robert E.] Rodes thinks that the <u>concepts</u> are self-exegeting under the heading of "nature," while you think that the <u>stories</u> are self-exegeting. I don't think that any one knot of the nexus is privileged, capable of freeing the dialogue from the relativity and vulnerability of actually listening, talking, and deciding. From where I stand, when Rodes says "nature is univocal," and you seem to say "story is univocal," although your answers are different, your methods seem to me both to make the same prior mistake, and in both cases the thesis loses me, leaving me to ask, "But what if it does not say that to me?" The univocality claim in either case leaves me out of the loop.

Because the people who claim to be doing serious moral theology refer to them, I have looked carefully recently at two specific stories. One is in the papers on "exceptions"... when black Methodist ethicist Major T. Jones cited Lutheran...Martin Marty, who cited Lutheran theologian/ethicist Joseph Sittler, who cited <u>The Cruel Sea</u> by novelist Monsarrat. The other is when several people, including former colleague (now lawyer) Leslie Griffin cited political philosopher Michael Walzer who cited existential philosopher-novelist Jean-Paul Sartre's <u>Dirty Hands</u>.

I go the second mile as Jesus said I should do.... I even go the third mile, trying to credit the sincerity of the citators and the authors, taking advantage of the fact that the Notre Dame Library has these story books, and I am still at a loss to understand on what grounds the whole chain of citators claims that some meaning is expressed, or validated, or clarified, or whatever, by those stories. Like many other stories, they might be taken as illustrating that some moral choices are difficult. What else is new? I didn't need to look hard for a far-out exceptional case, or a novelist who makes one up, to know that. Neither author of a fictional dilemma-case makes clear that the case proves anything about ethics, except that it is messy. That makes interesting fiction, but as moral discourse it is neither clear nor prototypical.

Just like other specimens of going the second mile, there is not always a payoff in terms of communication. I'll be polite, as befits an old cripple, and I won't say it in public, as befits a "sectarian" guest in a "Catholic establishment" culture, but so far nothing saves me from coming to the reluctant conclusion that my many third-mile hours spent trying to respect the Monsarrat-Sittler, Marty-Jones line, and the Sartre-Walzer-Griffin line, have been wasted on the use of dramatic stories to obfuscate. In your terms, of course, I could say that those are not good stories, or not about good people; but that purely formal description is petitionary, in the absence of a criteriology. (July 31, 1995)

Knowing How A Story Is Good

You say that you know a story is good before you test it by Scripture. I don't know how. You acknowledge the possibility of self-deception, but my criteria question is prior to that. Stanley [Hauerwas] says a lot about self-deception...but that does not help answer my question.

To say that finding a story good is an aesthetic question, like liking Mozart's music without approving of his lifestyle, may help to complicate our awareness that there are multiple criteriologies, but it does not help with my question. The parallel illustration of a painting which

(a) tells you something you didn't know, which

(b) you find to be true, does not parallel Mozart after all, and just rebegs the original question.

To say that a judgment is culturally conditioned, as you do, or that it is conditioned by its community setting, as does [Alasdair] MacIntyre, is true, and would matter if you were arguing with a pre-Enlightenment absolutist, but these statements only restate my question. In real human conflictual experience, either:

(a) you and I are in the same community and culture, and you want me to like your story, so that the platitudes fall away, or

(b) you and I are in different communities and/or cultures, but you want me to recognize that yours is better; then the platitudes are true, but you need a non-community-dependent warrant.

You say you have not argued that stories are self-exegeting or univocal. Maybe not overtly; yet you set up the pedagogical and dialogical processes as if they were. You point to them as answers or as criteria when I can see them only as illustrations, translations, instantiations.

Of course there is "something valid in stories, or I wouldn't use them." My question is not about whether but about how, subject to what discipline.

Telling a story is always a process of selection; what is said is naturally the easiest to justify in the Shafferian frame of "good stories about good people." What is left out? Does admiring Darrow as a defense attorney include pushing his fellow Tolstoyan Bryan into a fatal heart attack, if that is what happened? Can a story be morally good in your sense but be badly told in an aesthetic sense? I would have to assume so, and you would not mind. But then it would have to follow, wouldn't it, that a story can be morally bad but well told? How do you identify that one? Are there lawyer stories like that which are sold and read but which your canon rejects? Could/should there be a moral rating system, like for the movies?

I continue to want to assume that these questions could be answered, in a way which would retrieve the elements of the wider classical moral debate, rather than being dodged or begged. You seem to me to consider the "wider classical debate" as an adversary rather than as an ancillary resource, presumably because of some unpleasant experience in your youth with unredemptive use of imperatives. That, too, is a story, of course.

The reason you are at home with lawyer stories is partly that the courtroom setting as a macrocosm is much more orderly than the rest of the world; the sovereign is named and the rules have been developed to maximize fairness. Fine, that makes it work. But most of the morally important world is not like that. How would Atticus Finch operate in a system without fairness at the top? How would you tell the story of Hiroshima, or even of Waco, with a lawyer's eye? (August 16, 1995)

I don't know where you go for your criteria of "an intuitively persuasive story." I am not sure that all of the narratives I see you and Stanley building upon are "intuitively persuasive."[20] (May 1, 1993)

A problem Stanley does not help me with:

--...the use of fiction rather than real cases, without any sense of the

---

[20] I used as an epigraph for the chapter on stories in my Faith and the Professions (1987) a couple of sentences from the extensive literature on narrative of our friend Hauerwas: "Stories...are not told to explain as a theory explains, but to involve the agent in a way of life. A theory is meant to help you know the world without changing the world yourself; a story is to help you deal with the world by changing it through changing yourself." What I have had to say about narrative method in ethics makes me a more visible target for John's complaints, since I more than Stanley have, no doubt, made an epistemological defense of stories–stories as a way to know what is going on. The chapter for which I used Hauerwas as an epigraph makes that and other arguments.

Ethics and Eschatology

hermeneutics for knowing how a narrative constructed by an artist proves anything ethical....

--when the people who use a dramatic story, thinking it proves something about ethics, actually don't read it carefully, to see that it is not a case of what they take it for (namely killing ship-wrecked enemies when you have to, when the laws of war say you should fish them out of the water);

--when Major Jones cites Martin Marty citing Joseph Sittler citing Montsarrat as if there were something canonical about one particular war novel.

I do not "easily dismiss the single instance," because there is only one, or even because it is fiction, but because the whole <u>gestalt</u> of the argument stinks of bad faith, seeking more to undercut rules than to make them keepable.

Walzer is confusing about city bombing. He argues that the actual use of city bombing late in W.W.II was unjustified, yet he needs, in order to make his methodological point about dirty hands, to argue as if such massive bombing had been done early in the war, when Churchill was arguing that it would be (although immoral and illegal) necessary to win. Although he takes off from the real war, he departs from the reality [with a story?] to make a methodological argument.... (June 21, 1995)

Ethics of the Fitting

In Julia B. Meister's and my article on the use of the word "appropriate,"[21] we had been referred, by John and others, to the "ethics of the fitting" described by H. Richard Niebuhr[22] and Max Stackhouse, among others. I sent John a copy of our article:

Any notion of the "fitting" or the "unfitting" passes the buck definitionally, since it posits a frame of reference which it usually does not spell out. Yet it can be made accountable if the frame of reference is spelled out. To "fit" is always a context-dependent measure. In this sense it is a subset or functional equivalent of natural law, part of the identity of your institution [and of John's?]. It is also like your use of the appeal to "story"....

It would also help to compare/contrast "appropriate/inappropriate" with some of its rough synonyms. I just reread a statement by George Lindbeck, retired Yale theologian, saying that "the Biblical tolerance of slavery is now almost universally regarded by Christians as totally and permanently inapplicable." Reminds me of the press man in the Kennedy White House who said

---

[21] 46 <u>Duke Law Journal</u> 781 (1997).

[22] The leading source is, no doubt, Niebuhr's <u>The Responsible Self</u>.

that his statement of the previous day was now "inoperative." I think this was in the time of the Bay of Pigs.

The use of euphemisms to combine the air of firm discrimination with the looseness of definitional buck-passing is a phenomenon much broader than just the usage of one word. The entire "natural law" tradition has the same problem...as does your and Stanley's reliance on stories.

I was reminded of you this week by hearing a senator use "inappropriate" as the discriminating designation for certain fundraising practices.... (Undated, 1997)

John attended the annual meeting of the Editorial Board of the Journal of Law and Religion, in October, 1993, and a seminar in connection with it that had to do with the work of Professor Milner Ball, and with my work. His essay commenting on my work was in Volume Ten of that journal. He made notes during presentations–my own, Professor Ball's, and those of others; and some of these notes touched on story theology, an art demonstrated in Ball's work, particularly in his 1993 book The Word and the Law and in his Called by Stories (2000). From notes in John's file:

What is a good story...? Tacitly presupposes definitions and priorities–in conscience but unspoken **and** unconscious.... Not all stories are true–where is distinction? Stories read with rules and principles illuminate one another.... Stories are a more effective way to teach principles because (a) humanly empathic, (b) face cost-benefit complexity, (c) respect costly integrity, such rare cases as losing truthfully.... But what they teach is a separate question. Only what such a story teaches is right.

Quandary casuistry–stories are a way to test general rules as to how far they reach

--Punctualism[23] is mistake
--Stories are one way to restore discussion
--[Compare?] Pastoral/prophetic casuistry
        Priestly/Canonical....

---

[23] I read "punctualism" to mean "quandary ethics," which is the most common device of them all among teachers of legal ethics, and which I learned more about in Edmund Pincoffs's essay "Quandary Ethics," in Hauerwas's and MacIntyre's Revisions (1983). I criticized the law-teacher tendency in the introduction to my American Legal Ethics (1985). One of the claims of narrative method is that it overcomes the limitations of quandary ethics. Stanley Hauerwas's A Community of Character (1981) deals with this aspect of the method–and many others.

Ethics and Eschatology

Hero Stories

Professor Cathleen Kaveny also attended and participated in the J.L.R. 1993 seminar. Afterwards, John wrote her a letter about stories; from John's file copy:

I am most grateful for the privilege of having been invited last week into the special subculture of "the Law," and to have heard your response to Milner Ball.

What moves me to write is the sense that I both do and do not share your criticism of Ball's choice of hero stories.

As I said in my own remarks, to be in the category of narrative does not make a value testimony true. As Tom Shaffer later said orally, one must have "good stories of good people."

What makes a story "good" may be artistry, or perhaps the rarity or uniqueness of the event or person. What makes a person "good" needs other criteria. The virtue for the sake of which the story is valuable must be warranted by some criteria from outside the narration.

Take the case of Henry Schwartzschild [discussed in the 1993 Ball book]. That he is a good man shows in his Kantianism, in that the rightness of his opposition to capital punishment is independent of any provable success test. But what makes the story good in the former sense is the way Ball selected and wrote it, and the seldomness of a Jewish Kantian saving guilty lives.

Now if I got your critique of Ball correctly, you telescope the two kinds of goodness in your doubting the criterion that our life should be a parable of grace. You reject the tacit claim that each of us is called to be a Dorothy Day or an Atticus Finch, saying that God loves ordinary people too. There I agree. That is my doubt about the value (whether probative or parabolic/pedagogical) of farthest-out hero stories.

But then (here I go beyond your words) I remember your appeal to Barth III/4 seeming to say not merely "most people are not called to be heroes" but also "most people aren't called to be saints," linked perhaps to a shift in the balance between creation and redemption. This is a shift from "good" as in "good story" to "good" as in "good person." There I don't follow. The most ordinary or modest person is still called to be a parable of grace–though not a "good story."

This came back to mind when in another session you spoke of being professionally in an unreal ecological "bubble," so that a wise old person in the moot courtroom called you a candidate for burnout. That fact that you are not a hero, not tilting in vain against the death penalty, but rather doing ordinary careful paperwork for hospitals and courts, does not make you any less disciplined or industrious or hard on yourself. Ordinary people are still suffering servants.

In that session Greg Johnson advocated sabbaticals. I prefer the more elementary preventive, namely the Sabbath, i.e. a regular interruption of the grind, even the most urgent or righteous, and hope you can find a way to stop to breathe once a week. Yet my concern now is not that your health is my business, but that the way we who are not heroes nevertheless take our ordinary lives seriously indicates that "what is a good story" and "what is a good person" are separate debates.... (Yoder to Cathleen Kaveny, October 21, 1993)

Using Bible Stories

Part of the October, 1993, program was a discussion of a complaint I had made, in a Texas Law Review piece, about legal scholars who invoke biblical figures and biblical categories, such as "prophet," without disclosing whether they are serious or have only happened on a metaphor–as if they were using a bit of Egyptian mythology or a simile from Winnie the Pooh. It was a running discussion between Professor Howard Lesnick and me–some of which later got into print[24]–and between Professor Lesnick and Professor Emily Hartigan. After the event, John wrote to Professor Hartigan. From his file copy:

There is a more than whimsical attraction for me in your debate with Howard Lesnick about whether he does or does not believe what he says he does not. Once our ontology is loosened up, as people like Tom do, by putting stories in place of principles, then it can be argued that the whole universe of rules for how systems of ideas have to cohere comes loose.

The early Jewish Christians and their nonmessianic fellow Jews were taken by the Greeks and Romans to be "atheists" because the JHWH/kyrios/abba whom they honored could not be pictured or manipulated. I'm not sure that apart from the Jesus story we have a stake in "theism in general" as a reality stance which would either:

(a) be philosophically true independently of the salvation story, or

(b) be bigger than the salvation story and include it.

But then if a morally committed person like Howard, turned off by ontological word games and by oppression in the name of God, believes he can tell the true story without an a priori tip of the hat to any particular ontological superstructure, does that need to bother us?

Karl Rahner long ago proposed that Christian existence could be redefined in anthropological terms as responding to all of reality as gracious, and proceeded from there to offer to accredit as "anonymous Christians" anybody who

---

[24]Howard Lesnick, "Religious Particularity, Religious Metaphor, and Religious Truth: Listening to Tom Shaffer," 10 The Journal of Law and Religion 317 (1993-1994).

made that existential move even though it be made without the name of Jesus. That offer of unsolicited credentials was not widely accepted as a compliment by Buddhists and Hindus because it seemed patronizing. It seemed not to affirm the dignity of other faith postures in their own right. That does not however keep me from claiming Rahner's move as a ("catholic") precedent for giving less weight than Howard does to what he does with general theism.

A deeper criticism of Rahner's anthropological reduction (which I shall not go into here) is that it was more moral and psychological ("do you think the universe is friendly?") than moral (no enemy love, no renunciation of dominion).

But once we have accepted the MacIntyre/Hauerwas/Shaffer reduction to narrative, I do not see how to argue for the retention of yet a few more fragments of any traditional ontology. (Yoder to Professor Emily Hartigan, November 5, 1993)

John's October, 1993, file contained notes on Professor Ball's presentation, including the following. Some of these were later expanded in John's short essay in volume ten of the Journal of Law and Religion:

How to read a story is a different set of questions. The biblical stories are read in a believing community, providing norms for discussion that are anti-idol, anti-ideology, and anti-empire. What of Trollope's lawyer stories? [John's notes suggest that he admitted to being an outsider, but that he found a sense of irony in Trollope.] Any story is in some sense a deception, because it selects events and perspectives. [A related example is] lawyers' misuse of what they think of as legal history–e.g., on the federal constitution.

Caesar used narrative to kill, steal, and enslave.... [Stories supporting] racial superiority...Enlightenment rationality...[Inserted here:] Natural law is a problem area.

Open question: Is the loosening up which the narrative mode favors over against the rigidity also able to address critically the...products of an overtly cynical culture?

Seven ways--the thickness of the Hebraic substance tells us what good people are and even what a good story is:

--the rejection of idolatry
--the rejection of ideology
--the rejection of empire
--the affirmation of hope, which implies rejecting determinism
--partisanship for the underdog...
--refusal to let probable success be a decisive criterion...
--the affirmation of creativity, which explodes the dilemma bound quandaristic mood.

[P]articular stories stake their meaning from a master narrative which one holds or a given community holds to be the truest truth about the human condition. There are two primary nominees for that role in our culture. Both fit with the "Hebraic word." One of these is Diaspora: The people of God cultivate their identity in a world they do not control.... Let me call it the servant story.... Then there is the Christendom story...the meaning of history is borne by Caesar, and beginning with Constantine. (October 1993)

John's file contained undated notes on another and unrelated piece of his reading, on the Prophet Nathan: **"Story makes the point better but the principle defines the wrong."**

Dean Edward Gaffney and I both published essays in a book on the late Christian theologian and lawyer William Stringfellow. John's file contains notes he made on that book, and the following file copy of a memorandum he wrote to Gaffney and me:

Recent conversations in my Ph.D. seminar have led me to want to understand <u>as a syndrome</u> the phenomena common to Jacques Ellul, Stringfellow, Daniel Berrigan, Peter Maurin, and Francis Schaeffer. Each claims to be, and is in some ways, well informed about the history of the questions he speaks about with authority, even though he need not provide precise footnotes to validate that claim to erudition. Each gathered an admiring constituency of people from beyond our guild, quite different in membership from the fewer persons within the guild whose admiration is measured. Each claims in some way to be canonically accountable and bases arguments on his reading of particular biblical texts. Three of them make extensive use of <u>principalities and powers</u> language.

Comparing the above five men prompts one to ask questions about the sociology of knowledge. Why do people who make that kind of very confident idiosyncratic exegetical claim find a congenial audience more easily than more careful exegetes or historians of thought (like me) do? In the light of this correction, I see Gaffney and Shaffer as belonging in the above list.

On Lies

I gave a lecture at Hofstra University, on lying for clients, later published in a new ethics journal published at Hofstra, and at 71 <u>Notre Dame Law Review</u> 195 (1996). I used lots of stories in it; I depended on Aristotle's account of friendship; and I argued that an adequate understanding of the virtue of truthfulness lies more in our stories than in a principle or rule that would say, "Do not tell a lie." John gave me some ideas:

I have been wondering for decades what the rules are for knowing (a) what is a good story and (b) what a story teaches. The longer you go on the less I can follow.

You think I am asking rigorously for exceptionless rules, since some of the professionals in the field do. I think on the other hand that I want to know more

about each of the stories in order to evaluate why you think they prove what you think they prove.

You have a prior definition of what is a lie that seems to me to be part of the rigor you purport to want to overcome, judging ancient near eastern tricksters [the matriarch Rebecca and the prophet Elisha] by rules foreign to their genre.

But the place you most often lose me is the preference for friend over enemy; you mitigate it at some points, and cite Jesus, but the structure of most of the argument still uses "help your friends" as a principle, and quandaries as exception-makers.

Most of the prohibitions of the decalogue stand in for the dignity of the Other, whom I will harm if I prefer myself, of which my friends are a part. The dignity of the legal process which keeps you from approving lying to a lawyer stands in for the dignity of the Other; I don't see the rationality (in your terms) of telling the adversary lawyer the truth, but I agree. The judge even more; whereas the adversary lawyer is your peer, fellow officer of the court, the judge is not just a lawyer who happens to be on the bench; he represents on the next higher level the right of the Other to a fair process.

If I were assigned to facilitate a wider dialogue, rather than just respond to this thesis, I would look for other elements of the long story rather than center on the methodological debate in which we accuse each other of having principles.

I would review the moral theologians for whom lying is different from killing, so that even in a just war you must not lie. This tradition includes Augustine, canon lawyer Charles Mackwey of Rome in the 1911 <u>Catholic Encyclopedia</u>, George Orwell, and Robert Rodes. In general I learn more from attempting to unpack the dignity of positions I disagree with than from applauding my friends, and this is one of the classical ones. Back in that history there are notions of Truth as divine, of the dignity of the person I am speaking to as the Divine Image, which seem to me to be of another order of magnitude from the finite pragmatic stakes in the stories you cite.

On the other side of the debate I would review my reasons for thinking that once the Allies were committed to killing as many Germans as possible, the strategies whereby they led the Nazi commanders not to expect the invasion in the right place were part of the deal. If Eisenhower had radioed Hitler, "We are going to invade Normandy," it would not have been believed. When there is a basic readiness to destroy one another, I would honor the strategist who would draw some line on his own idiosyncratic moral grounds (like Stimson saying "gentlemen don't read each other's mail"), but I would not build a case, as you say [Sisela] Bok does [in her book on lies], on what is lying, out of such massive constructions of reciprocal deception. A larger problem for me would be the spymasters who sent their own people (British spies, and their French contacts) to certain death, lying to them about their mission, in order to keep on deceiving the Germans. Even more I would think it should be a larger problem for your way of favoring friends.

Lastly, I would look more to the social matrix, as more than individual. Your answer is "identify your friend, remember that you are a gentleman, and do what seems right." Mine would be, "Take account of all the parties in the process." That would include the human dignity of the adversary, the social dignity of the informal and formal conflict management process, and the awareness of my own selfish bias. I think this phrasing renders more deeply the meaning which H. Richard Niebuhr's purely formal slogans are capable of. It includes room for "put yourself in the other person's place," and for "if it is right for you is it right for others?" as tests.

I am surprised how much came to mind after deciding not to discuss the stories; sorry for the bulk. Enjoy yourself at Hofstra. (June 25, 1995)

Narrative in Scripture

To Hear the Word includes John's acceptance of a narrative theology as a way to re-tell his learning from Scripture. When I read this for the first time, in the fall of 2001, I wished, as I often have, that I could revive a conversation....

"**The category of story and the claim of that story to be rooted in real people and places distinguishes Christian faith from most other religions before and since. That faith is therefore documented not primarily in visions or in speculative theories about divine reality, but in narratives and pastoral letters which claim to be testimonies to the norming process within an ongoing community. That is how they claim to have been written and that is how we should best take them.... All of the tests show the process of taking the Jesus of the story as the norm. That is the Jesus of history (what really happened) as mediated by real history (the traditioning process of the community), rather than the Jesus of modern skeptical historiography.... (94-95)**

"**It is appropriate that the form in which the impact of Jesus is mediated is first of all a series of narratives and of oral interpretations of narrated events, and that that tradition should be available in the form of first-century literature, nearly contemporary with the events it points to but not quite." (p. 109)**

"**It is more often the case (though seldom avowed) that the critic disagrees not with the claim that it is formally possible to do ethics in the light of the Scriptures, but rather with the conclusions which are reached when that is done. The critic says, 'You can't really take the Bible seriously,' meaning that when it is accountably interpreted it says things which she or he does not want to believe or to obey, like affirming the necessity of suffering, or poverty, or love of enemy. If the most convinced and competent ethical exegete were coming up with less offensive guidance (e.g., with the validation of mid-American patriotic culture, or** with a blank check for whatever cause our particular group happens to believe in), then very few would say, 'You can't do that with the Bible.' It is when the original message projects a moral style which is uncomfortable and counter-cultural that colleagues and communities discover that it is methodologically naive to read it that way." (p. 112)

D. FEMINIST JURISPRUDENCE

Professor Clare Dalton, in a talk during the 1992 annual meeting of the Association of American Law Schools, gave as an instance of feminist jurisprudence the fact that all members of a class of third-grade children, dealing with one of their number who was deaf, learned sign language:

Can what Prof. Dalton described about helping a deaf child work for other subjects as well? Could it possibly work to protect a minority child against imposed prayers in public schools? N.B.C.T.V. news this Sunday (while I was reading your text) reported a Texas high school where a senior (a Lutheran, not a Jew or an atheist) had to use the courts to keep the school from imposing a form of prayer on him. Could the students do for that what Dalton's children did for deafness? ... The Dalton story about sign language reminds me of the very broad use Stanley [Hauerwas] has made of the difference between the U.K. and the U.S.A. on whether to pay people to give blood. (Dec. 29, 1992)

Private Sex

[Is sex private?] To link sex with family including children is right but I don't think it [identifies] the basic betrayal. Prior to separating sex from childbearing is separating it from reciprocity and monogamy. By definition the only private sex is lonely masturbation. The point is that sex (which is never private) has become free to be nonreciprocal and nonmonogamous. The children may well be, in terms of anthropology and sociobiology, the reason reciprocity and monogamy are functional, but a couple staying together "because of the children" is not good for the children. (April 20, 1993)

Working for Women

[On a report of my experience in a legal-aid office managed by women:] I am glad to hear that, in one setting, your experience with feminine management has been different and better.... That fits my picture of primitive matriarchy and with Jesus as feminist. That does not set aside the fact that for the first years the typical infant experiences the typical mother as omnipotent, and that sometimes that control is used to make the child yield (for his own good, of course) to her will. Nor are women incapable of fury (the Eumenides, the Bacchae).

Some of the caucusing of politicized feminists these days is no less punitive than men. When a man is angry, taking the primitive model of the hunt or battle, he grants that the adversary is a peer doing his same thing, sometimes by the rules. When a mother punishes, the child has no peer status, since the mother's benevolence is <u>a priori</u> unchallengeable. He will get the breast or the bottle only by totally yielding.

In the short story "The Lottery," the victim (that year) was a woman, and a man ran the drawing, but the first two people to pick up stones were women, and the drawing could have hit the father or the son in the family as well. In other scapegoating rituals gathered by [Rene] Girard (or by Frazer before him) the victim has to be a man; also in the Bacchae and potentially in the Eumenides.

The work setting like the one you testify to is the last place I would expect "maternal control," of the punitive type I describe, to operate. There are strongly functional role definitions and little for anyone to gain by pulling rank, and no room simply to coerce. Thus, while I am glad for your good experience with female administration, I doubt that it sets aside my point. (May 1, 1993)

Chapter Four

On the Possibility of a Christian Law School

Several of the pieces John helped me with (and in one case my mentor Bob Rodes and me) involved arguments for a Christian law school, and analysis and criticisms of American law schools that claim, or at one time claimed, a Christian religious heritage. When I wrote on this subject in an essay in the <u>Stanford Law Review</u> (1993) I counted 46 accredited law schools in the U.S. that claimed church affiliation and two that claimed to be Jewish. (The force of "accredited" here is that the graduates of these schools are, after graduation, eligible to seek licenses to practice law.) The essay attempted to defend a separation of these schools into three ecclesiological categories:

    (i) <u>secular</u>: The church affiliation is historical, formal, functionally irrelevant--at most administrative; I argued that this category included most church-affiliated schools.

    (ii) <u>Erastian</u>: The church affiliation is significant and even vital, but "under the Erastian position, the Church serves a civil society that remains, in important ways, Christian"; I argued that this position has been common among Roman Catholic law schools.

    (iii) <u>sectarian</u>: "The peculiar calling of the people of God is to be distinct within civil society and to endure consequent separation from it." This position, like the Erastian, assumes "that a law school maintained by a church can be one of the manifestations of the church in the world, and that such a manifestation is the principal reason the church has a law school." The position is, I thought then (and still think), hypothetical. There are no sectarian law schools. (I would be willing to talk, though, about the Reuben J. Clark Law School at Brigham Young University.)There are in any event no Anabaptist law schools.

These positions were discussed, in a sometimes lively fashion, in a meeting at the law school at Pepperdine University (Churches of Christ), in February 2002, of an association of religiously affiliated schools. This association has been in relatively informal existence for about 20 years.

John dealt with all three concepts when he and I discussed the law (and at other times as well).

I disagree with the thesis that academic religion doubts [whether a lawyer can be a good person--a familiar way to state an issue in academic legal ethics]. Many academic religionists are sorry they are not in law. They romanticize what law can do. You remember once meeting Mennonite lawyers and law students who thought they could not be Mennonite Christians. [Well, they kept the question alive.] You have cited me, correctly, as asking, maieutically, whether a Christian is called to law, but I ask the same question about farming or banking or the clergy or academic religion. My point in asking the maieutic question is to get people to ask not "yes or no?" but "under what conditions and with what understanding?" ... The Pauline understanding of ministry assigns to everyone a role in the body of the church. The view you apply to law is the Reformation doctrine of vocation, and I support it; it is just a different point from Paul on charisma. The two are not in conflict.... (Dec. 29, 1992)

A. THE LAW SCHOOL IN THE CHURCH

Robert E. Rodes, Jr., and I, in talks at the law schools at Notre Dame and at the University of Dayton, both Roman Catholic institutions, and subsequently in a published article,[25] argued that the way for our part of higher education to be Christian was to think of the law school as part of the church--Rodes arguing from the Vatican II document <u>Gaudium et Spes</u>, and I arguing a bit more from an ecclesiology that referred to the Radical Reformation, a position I have been willing to have called "sectarian." Yoder helped us with the draft, and then Yoder and I continued the conversation:

[Milner S. Ball's] description of Henry Schwarzschild ...seems to me sufficient refutation of the idea that it would not be possible to do legal education or legal action from a "sectarian" position. Henry is a Kantian in law, in that he disregards the criterion of success and continues to oppose wrongdoing even when

---

[25] 14 Dayton Law Review 5 (1988).

On the Possibility of a Christian Law School

he has little chance of winning. His late brother, my good friend [Rabbi Professor Steven Schwarzschild], was a Kantian in the philosophical sense for similar reasons but even more rigorously, since he taught philosophy. To be Kantian is not for me the Gospel, but it does state, in terms that Enlightenment people are used to listening to, the thesis that moral values are not dependent upon cultural consensus about their existence or about how successful one's life will be if lived in conformity to them. (July 31, 1995)

I would use "sectarian" only in square quotes, in the awareness that most current usage gives it a meaning which is not only pejorative but wrong. I accept its use when accountably defined to mean a group holding to values not derived from the majority: like Catholics honoring the pope or rejecting abortion. I reject its use when it is taken to mean disrespect for dialogue or thinking one has all the truth, or making contrariness a style commitment. (Nov. 5, 1997)

When you say [that by using] "church" you mean "the believing people of God," that is biblical, but not very Roman Catholic. For the [law graduates] your model proposes to send out to function in the world, in the roles you describe, sacerdotal hierarchy or the centrality of the eucharist are not constitutive. Political/moral definition is, and that is what you derive from Jesus. Jesus renounces the power models of the Romans and of the Zealots, but he does not renounce the power of truth-telling, of servanthood, of community.... Your listeners probably think that the originality of the projected alumni's projected performances would be making a point of working cleanly within the rules of the guild, rather than corruptly at the edge. But your argument, if more explicit, would relativize the whole notion of guild.....

Once you have made your definition of "church" (=synagogue), in terms that fit the early Christians or the Radical Reformation, who will build the bridge between that and the various ways Roman Catholics define "church"? Whether it be the vision of Bishop [John] D'Arcy, of Richard McBrien, of [Hans] Kung, or of [Cardinal] Ratzinger, none of them would connect easily with your answer. (Nov. 6, 1997)

Religious Vocation On the Law Faculty

You imagine a school which would take the liberty of costing less by using the devoted services of committed faculty. You did not need to imagine from scratch.... Countless Christian schools have done that in other disciplines. When I was at Goshen [College] in the 1940s they argued with the N.C.A. that the salary differential between Mennonite faculty there and what those same people could earn at Northwestern should be counted as part of the N.C.A. calculation of the school's economic viability. The earliest higher schools in all disciplines of early modern Europe, like the earliest hospitals, were monastic. Obviously students would not be half sold out to the rat race when they graduate if you made the tuition free by using donated services.

Next question: If you had that kind of sacrificial integrity, would you also provide that free education to students who did not share the vision?

You say [with some satisfaction that] the American Bar Association has fits because of the challenge of respecting irreducible "sectarian" schools that are small and embattled, and being challenged as to what constitutes "quality." But something else is involved when you include Pat Robertson, with his big, well-financed operation brought whole from Tulsa [Oral Roberts University], part of his campaign for the presidency. A sect which is planning to take over the Republican Party and then the U.S.A. and then the world should not be set in parallel with the early Christians. There are similarities in the social setting within American pluralism, between Virginia Beach [Rev. Robertson's law school–now called Regent] and Buies Creek [Campbell College], but there are also weighty contrasts as to the substance of what it means for each of them, morally and politically, to affirm [Rodes's phrase] the transcendence of the person.

Do you mean that the American Bar Association should not be able to learn or mature beyond the convulsive stage, so that honoring little value-biased schools will always scandalize them, or would there be <u>valid</u> quality criteria which such schools ought to be asked to meet, more than just sacrificial devotion? Example: Bob Jones University, rejecting racial integration (at the cost of sacrificing tax exemption). If they taught that in a law school, would you plead their case before the A.B.A.? (April 26, 1994)

Ecclesiology is a promising [place to begin], because it bypasses post-establishment post-Christian categories in favor of simpler biblical categories....

One of the differences between the description and the norm is the one you made obvious: The real track record of Catholic law schools is considerable success in pursuing a different, quite specific, well defined goal, namely the professional advance of the grandchildren of immigrant Irish, Italians, Poles, and Bavarians. A deeper question which you did not label is the one represented sacramentally by the traditional practice of infant baptism:

If you were to take seriously the perspective of the New Testament and the early centuries, being gently renewed today by Catholic sacramental theologians like Aidan Cavanagh and William Storey, then the only people [lawyers] who can be counted on to be the "church," in the normative sense..., are the ones who voluntarily ask for it. That commitment to discipleship cannot be the guaranteed product of a curriculum or even of the impact of charismatic teachers...if it is not part of the conditions for entering or leaving the school.

That does not mean it should not be the stated goal. It does not mean that the skills it calls for cannot be named and modeled. But following Jesus is, he himself warned (Luke 14:25ff), not a normal thing to decide to do. Some people

On the Possibility of a Christian Law School

have made that choice; some clearly have not. The fuzziness of the categories, i.e.,
--that some have made it but are inconsistent;
--that some have not but are sometimes decent;
--that some are undefined;
does not change the fact, on the principled level, that some people are and some are not addressable in virtue of their baptismal vows (or functional equivalent). That is the ecclesiological question which your model does not name. Not that you could not have, but then it would be even more threatening.

Suppose this: The presence of the law school ought to be the presence of the power of truth and love in the interest of the truth and the neighbor rather than the power of.... Would it make your point more clear? Or would the clarity take the edge off of a paradox which you need to keep? (Feb. 22, 1989)

To Turn From Membership to Meaning

In <u>Body Politics</u> (p. 74), John answered in the following way the question of how the gospel "impinges on the rest of our world": "[W]e can afford to begin with the gospel notions themselves and then work out from there...rather than beginning with the 'real world' out there (someone else's definition of 'the nature of things') and then trying to place the call of God within it."

He had written, in 1955, in the <u>Mennonite Quarterly Review</u>, in an essay reprinted in <u>The Royal Priesthood</u>: "There is no such thing as an isolated word of the Bible carrying meaning in itself. It has meaning only when it is read by someone and then only when that reader and the society in which he or she lives can understand the issue to which it speaks." (pp. 38-39)

He interpreted the development of Dr. King's thought in these communal terms. In an essay called "Three Unfinished Pilgrimages," in <u>Faith and Freedom</u> (1993), John spoke of King's early years as being devoted to a sort of politics of nonviolence. As he came to oppose the War in Viet Nam and to campaign for fair housing in Chicago, though, King demonstrated "a growing awareness that the people of God whose dreams he spoke for was both smaller than and larger than America. He began to preach that 'We shall overcome' is not true without the cross...." He "began to be aware of a need to discern the difference between the committed community of disciples and the wider society within which the church testifies and which the church calls to faith. A distinguishable believing community is the prerequisite for a pattern of moral thought in which Jesus Christ (rather than some lesser value like the well-being of the nation) is the norm, and for a nonviolent social ethic." (p. 17, vol. 2)

[Your] scenario[26] [imagining a law school growing within a primitive Christian community], growing from letting one of one's members get into the law to creating one's own school, is logical, as unfolded out of the social posture of ancient Jewry and early Christianity. What strikes me is a set of questions which do not arise:

--This <u>would be a way</u> for the church to develop into accepting the profession and then training for it. So an authentic non-domineering church (or synagogue) could with integrity take that path. But if she did, what kind of school would it be? How would it differ from the one Notre Dame actually has, based as it is on other rationales and other precedents? Where would the function be located if keeping in touch with the student, to see that she does not sell out to the pagan values of the environing culture?

--Would this be any different from why the church should have a medical school, or a school of education, or a school of business, or a Reserve Officers Training Corps? The argument being largely formal, I should think it would apply across the spectrum. The law may be the queen of the professions, but the argument should not apply only there.

--On what grounds would the early community decide <u>which</u> professions would not be approved, or for which approved professions the community should not try to run its own schools? That could be because the difference that faith makes for a particular profession is not important, or because the cost is not manageable, or because the guild will not let believers in. (When you were an A.B.A. accreditor, was there anything you would <u>not</u> accredit?)[27]

--Is Bob [Rodes's] criterion of "transcendence of the human person" an adequate surrogate for all the dimensions of the difference faith makes? Or is it the core of a much larger skein of indispensable functional traits? If [the campus leaders] used that as criterion, would "the Catholic character" of Notre Dame be safe? (January 20, 1993)

---

[26] I was accused of being "Yoderian" when I presented this idea at a conference held in New York City, at a center presided over by Richard John Neuhaus and sponsored by the Rockefeller Foundation. A revised version of it is in the last chapter of my daughter's and my 1991 book <u>American Lawyers and Their Communities</u>.

[27] In my six years on the Accreditation Committee of the Section on Legal Education and Admissions to the Bar, of the A.B.A., the only law schools that had difficulties, in the arena John identified, were those that were regarded as "sectarian." None of the 28 Roman Catholic schools had any difficulty. The Mormon, Pentecostal, and Southern Baptist schools did.

On the Possibility of a Christian Law School

The Significance of Capital Punishment

A passing consequence of our conversation was a letter from Yoder to the Dean of the Notre Dame Law School, copy to me. I also found a copy in John's files:

[I]t would seem to me that somewhere in the world of Catholic law schools in this country, whether in one of them functioning on behalf of the wider community, or in some federative modality, there would be a focusing of competences upon the necessary educational and institutional struggle which it will take to get the U.S.A. to hear and respect this witness [against the death penalty], in which the Catholic position agrees with the ("natural") insights of most modern societies but differs with the way our own country is currently going.

As a layman, I would think this would call for focusing attention on finding the resources for the defense of the accused. Many of them get only pro-bono attorneys who are not strongly resourced and usually not experienced in the field. I would think there could and should be a literature service, seminars, maybe even a hot line, where counsel assigned to capital cases could get the best help.

Obviously, such expertise would have to include keeping in touch with the changing legislative and judicial picture in all of the diverse jurisdictions.

Some of this kind of service is rendered, expertly, on a shoestring, by the National Coalition to Abolish the Death Penalty. But what Catholic liaison do they have? I would think that there should be routinely assured Catholic support from law schools for that work, in staff and funding, but also by giving their work visibility in the curriculum....

As a moral theologian, I can see both strengths and drawbacks in the hierarchy's having englobed capital punishment with other kinds of killing under the rubric "seamless robe" or "consistent ethic." From a pastoral and pedagogical perspective, on the other hand, that linkage represents a powerful moral commitment and would (it seems to me, as a resident alien within the Catholic culture) call for wide backing for this kind of special educative focus.

In addition to helping lawyers to defend capital cases, there should be a basis in Catholic colleges for turning the public opinion around, as it seems to be drifting rather in the wrong direction recently.

If I understand aright, the importance of the networking to provide defendants with competent counsel would be not only for the sake of the unique intrinsic value of those accused individuals' lives, but also that energetically arguing every case is one of the best ways to educate our public, not only for <u>general</u> sensitivity to the evil of killing killers, but also to the dimensions of race and class discrimination, fallibility, and the killing of innocents....

If there ought to be some such center in some Catholic law school, some could say that it should be in the federal capital, and then we could "let

George(town) do it." But most of the jurisdictions which kill people are not federal. Maybe it should be Tulane, since Louisiana is especially rough. But Indiana is also a death penalty state, [with] some dramatically visible cases, and Notre Dame has a self-image which would be compatible with investing in providing leadership in the field.

This vision would be compatible with the kind of leadership currently envisioned for the human-rights center...but it could be more narrowly targeted. When I asked Tom Shaffer where in the American Catholic legal-education system this concern is lodged, he said "nowhere." Would this not be a fitting challenge for your school to take on? Perhaps in concert with the bishops' conference. (Mid-May 1993, letter to Dean David T. Link, "cc: Shaffer")

One of the paradoxes around Notre Dame is the peculiar way Catholics have of honoring saints without following them; e.g., the role of Dorothy Day or Mother Teresa. They do that with modern "saints," because their intellectual tradition is to do it with Jesus. They agree with [Reinhold] Niebuhr that Jesus's humanity is symbolic absolute purity but not real history. Then my agreeing to accept in the name of the peace churches, or of Jesus, the honor of recognition for that kind of sanctity, the sanctity of otherworldly purity or irrelevance, would be to play along with a misunderstanding of the ordinariness, the real-world historicity, i.e., the normativeness, of the power of love. (Feb. 22, 1989)

A Bit More Detail On Being Sectarian

I have tended, in law-school essays, to deal calmly with the designation "sectarian," as Stanley Hauerwas sometimes does: John, as usual, wanted to know what was going on:

Until Troeltsch, the term was pejorative. It meant many people who think they have the truth. Secondly, but only derivatively, it meant people who, since the truth they have is not accepted, are willing to accept in turn that they should be shut out of the social process. Only with Troeltsch, followed by a generation of Anglo-Saxon sociology researchers, did the notion come to be given a more descriptive and less pejorative tonality. It could mean simply a free church or a voluntarily constituted community, and [thus] the sociologists describing and interpreting its activities did not have to involve negative overtones.

Unfortunately, what has happened in recent years is a return to the pejorative use. Although Helmut Richard Niebuhr followed Troeltsch in trying to use the term descriptively, considering that that posture was one which ought to be represented in the ecumenical mix, Niebuhr's pupil James Gustafson has returned to the pejorative usage and has applied it especially to George Lindbeck and Stanley Hauerwas.[28] You are therefore entering something of a conceptual minefield when you pick up the term as if it has a standard usage that could be considered objective and acceptable to the people whom it describes.

All of the above is further complicated of course by the sassy and paradoxical way in which our friend Stanley used the pejorative terms in self-description. The place where these two questions of terminology overlap is that I am thought of as interpreting the position called "sectarian," [although] I cannot accept it being assumed that I deny a kind of concern for the rest of the world which you follow Bob [Rodes] in assigning to the Erastians.... [T]here is nothing about the ethics I teach which ever accepts a priori not being heard by the wider world. We always assume that, the truth we proclaim being true, everybody ought to hear it and if they heard it and listened their lives would be better. What we [also] accept is that, a posteriori, we can go on living with the fact that we will not be heard, whereas the Erastian (or Constantinian) position actually becomes incoherent in a setting where you cannot rule. (Jan. 20, 1993)[29]

[It is odd the way some people] take for granted that we know the

---

[28] John dusted off an old essay, updated it, and contributed it and other material to a volume directed at H. Richard Niebuhr's typology, in Stassen, Yeager, and Yoder, <u>Authentic Transformation: A New Vision of Christ and Culture</u> (1996). He and James Gustafson squared off a bit at one another (a bad metaphor here, I guess–but I plead that I was present and heard them both) in a conference at Washington and Lee in 1985, published in Harlan R. Beckley and Charles M. Swezey (eds.), <u>James M. Gustafson's Theocentric Ethics: Interpretations and Assessments</u> (1988). John's phrase for part of the title to his contribution there–"the burden of a particular identity"–is, I think, a nice way to think about the issue of sectarianism.

[29] A less sassy treatment by Hauerwas is in his Nancey Murphy's and Mark Nation's <u>Theology Without Foundations: Religious Practice and the Future of Theological Truth</u> (1994). John had contrasted, in an unpublished paper Hauerwas quoted in an essay published in 1980, Reinhold Niebuhr's universalism with his own. Niebuhr, Yoder said, "wants to be taking responsibility for and giving meaning to the cultural mainstream." John would, by contrast, trust in the Lordship of God and therefore "that his power and goodness can reach beyond the number of those who know him by his right name. The former universalism is a high view of the human; the latter is a high view of Jesus."

difference between "narrow" and "broad" meanings of the word "sectarian".... [I]t is useful to distinguish between an epistemological meaning, which says that only our group knows the truth, and a sociological meaning, which says that the people of God has an identifiable membership which is not the same as the whole society. That description is not only definable but enables one to interpret what Troeltsch was about and what would still make a difference for speaking to government or running a law school....

Categories of H. Richard Niebuhr [Christ and Culture] were enormously misleading, as I have been saying for almost thirty years.... Niebuhr has a respectable position, but it is deceptive when he clothes it in a typology which also claims to be non-judgmental and empirical. (May 20, 1993)

John noted, in an essay entitled "Gospel Renewal and the Roots of Nonviolence" (Faith and Freedom, December 1995) that the Radical Reformation rested on two principles, in addition to those of the "magisterial" Reformation: (i) "[P]resent agencies are not qualified to reform themselves" and (ii) "the movement called upon to undergo reformation has a normative foundation within history, which it is possible to deny and therefore also possible to reaffirm.... Waldo, Chelcicky, the Zurich radicals in 1523, George Fox in the 1640s, Alexander Campbell, William Booth, and Uchimura Kanzo each had his own focal agenda, local and different each time. Yet within a generation each had brought into being a community marked by voluntary membership, independence from the state, lay Bible study, shared leadership, economic sharing, and the rejection of war."

Looking at that sort of community from a political (and legal) perspective, he wrote in an essay entitled "Liberating Must Come First: Exodus Precedes Sinai" (1972), is a matter of confirming the identity of a minority: "The form of liberation in the Biblical witness is not the guerrilla campaign against an oppressor culminating in his assassination and military defeat but the creation of a confessing community which is viable without or against the force of the state, and does not glorify that power structure even by the effort to topple it. The content of liberation in the biblical witness is not the 'nation-state' or the 'class-state' brotherhood engineered after the take-over but the covenantal peoplehood already existing because God has given it...."

"Fundamentalist"

You attempt to be fair in the use of the word "Fundamentalist" and some of your sources are people trying to be fair, but you have no one to quote who likes the word. Jerry Falwell accepted the term and used it as the title for a glossy monthly magazine which he operated for a while. His definition would not be very different from...Carl Henry's, but it might strengthen the credibility of your documentation to cite someone who likes the word for himself. (Jan. 20, 1993)

B. LEGAL ORDER

I suggested in a draft of a talk on "Religion in the Life of a Lawyer," at Fordham, in June, 1997, that the Radical Reformation lesson for Christian lawyers--and perhaps for Jews--is that religion subverts legal order:[30]

As usual, I am in overall agreement with your agenda.

Instead of me you quote an anonymous Mennonite lawyer. It is good not to be the only person quoted....

I just got a copy of a review done by Nicolas Wolterstorff, whom you must know (Calvinist philosopher from Calvin College, sometime Notre Dame guest, now at Yale), on my Priestly Kingdom. I only skimmed it, and must return to learn from it with more care, but his idea seems to be, in line with the standard Calvinist mode of putting Anabaptists in the "against culture" box, that I always oppose the created order and never bless it, whereas one should be more discriminating, blessing the good and critiquing the bad. Isn't your bias for subversion subject to the same caricature?

What Huldryck Zwingli thought (or at least what he said) in October 1523 was not that the state should decide on theological truth but that "milords" of the Council were responsible to determine the modalities of implementation. The "disputation" which was drawing to a close had determined (a) that we should not worship images and (b) that the Eucharist is not a sacrifice. The question was how now to implement those two Reformed insights in the practice of the parishes of Zurich. He agreed with Stumpf that "milords" should not rule on theology. It is not clear that either Stumpf or Conrad Grebel (more vocal in the event) disagreed with Zwingli at that time. They lost confidence in him when six weeks later it became clear that "modalities of implementation" could include considerable delay in doing what he had already agreed was imperative....

My reading of [pacifism among] Jews is that while not explaining it in terms of Christian discipleship, practically all Jews from Jeremiah to Hertzl were not willing to kill for the government. The Maccabees and the Zealots were tiny exceptions which happened to get the limelight by happening in the Holy Land, but most Jews did not support them. Nor did most goy governments want the Jews to be armed. Only after [the] Enlightenment did Jews start thinking it was a good thing to become citizens (e.g. Dreyfus). (May 13, 1997)

Best wishes for you keynoting at Fordham on behalf of a Jewish lawyer. [Professor Russell Pearce organized the event, but maybe John was referring to

---

[30]Published at 70 Fordham Law Review 1857 (2002).

Jesus.]

My ecclesiology is quite analogous to that of Jews from Jeremiah to Hertzl; of them what you say about "subversion," as a byproduct of faithfulness rather than as an end in itself, would run in parallel....

Your use of [Walter] Brueggemann is significant, because he is a Calvinist. As is seen in [Richard] Mouw and Wolterstorff, Calvinism is also subversive in the sense you describe. Huguenots against Catholic France, William of Orange against Catholic Spain, and then his descendant of the same name taking over England. It is a mistelling of history to say that it was the Anabaptists who had a theological recipe for unrest.

There is a conference going on right now in Oxford about the thought of theological lawyer Wm. Stringfellow. People have asked me why in [Andrew] McThenia's book about Stringfellow both you and Ed Gaffney digress from Stringfellow to quote me (from letters which I don't find in the file). One reason for me to publish less would be that other people do it for me, but then only in odd snippets for their own purposes. What with [Jefferson] Powell and Stanley [Hauerwas] and theodicist (N.D. alumnus) Charles Pinchas using my letters, I should either stop writing such epistles, or begin writing a book entitled "how you got me wrong." At least Bryan Hehir has not quoted the 17-page critique of the second draft of the Bishops' peace pastoral which I sent him in 1982. (May 23, 1997)

The Sacraments

You say that Bob Rodes says that the reason for denying religious liberty to Anabaptists was that the persecutors wanted to save the babies from limbo. True on the surface but to do that you don't need to kill the parents; just use a fire hose on the kids, since parental consent was not part of the validity of the sacrament.

The magisterial reformers were not concerned for the babies and hell since their doctrine of baptism was not thus linked with the hereafter. Their reason was that if you leave baptism up to the individual, and some choose not to request it, they will not be good citizens, since you will have no hold on them. The spiritual togetherness of the corpus christianum was weightier than the eternal destiny of individuals. Both Luther and Zwingli believing in double predestination, where the soul ends up is not something we can administer in any case.

Speaking of the validity of sacraments, I just had a Ph.D. student write a paper claiming to prove that it made a difference that Margaret Sanger was baptized Roman Catholic in infancy. He quoted the modern catechism on indelibility. The exposition never got back to what difference it made. Would an unbaptized Margaret Sanger have been a better or worse person? Would her advocacy of family planning, or of relatively free love, or her eugenics, have been any different in social impact or in any other way than if her only very thinly affiliated mother had not had her done as a child? Wanting to save her from limbo was hardly the reason. (May 23, 1997)

The Emperor Constantine and H. Jefferson Powell

In a memo John wrote me about commenting on Jefferson Powell's book on constitutionalism, during a "conversation" we had at the Notre Dame Law School, on Powell's work and on his use of John's theology:

What I find most challenging is not the texture of a debate going on within a given arena, whether a real world arena like law, commerce, or an intellectual one, but the point at which people at home in one arena settle prematurely on a limited agenda. (March 6, 1998)

[John's notes, taken during that "conversation" include:] **A theory without belief is like a joke; if much is at stake you turn away from the truth.... Lawyers when they talk about law speak of <u>rules</u> but when they <u>do</u> law there are not rules but only a "vast surround" of texts.... The central texts contain assertions that there is no capacity to read or write authoritative texts; they have kept the badge to themselves.... [A play on a figure suggested to the "conversation" by Professor Joseph Vining:] The figure of a man in the corner of a room who says that he is not there and you are blind.**[31]

One participant's remarks, in a conversation that included many references to the Emperor Constantine, provoked John to write me a memo, separate from the notes he made, and separate from his formal comments on Powell's book, which are in the published account of the conversation:

That the meaning of "Constantine" belongs on the level of legend rather than that of history was well documented in the midst of a recent event at the Notre Dame Law School. In response to the pejorative reference to Constantine as symbol in H. Jefferson Powell's <u>The Moral Tradition of American Constitutionalism</u> (Durham, Duke, 1993), one participant, who shall be nameless here because in his own field he is very competent, said that Constantine "ended persecution and saved the lives of hundreds of thousands of Christians." That is simply false. Galerius, who had ordered the last wave of persecution, already suspended it before he resigned, because it was not working. Even before he suspended it, the order of magnitude of the operation was never in the thousands. Licinius, Constantine's fellow-Caesar, had confirmed the same measure (the number of Christians in his Eastern part of the empire was greater than in the West) before Constantine joined

---

[31] The Notre Dame conversation on Powell's book is reported at 72 <u>Notre Dame Law Review</u> 11 (1996). Professor Vining's contribution is at pp. 15-27.

him in the Edict of Milan. Nor did Constantine believe in full tolerance. He soon mobilized state resources against the dissident Donatists in North Africa, and only relaxed those measures when he in turn learned that they were unenforceable. (May 1996)

John contributed an essay called "Primitivism in the Radical Reformation: Strengths and Weaknesses" to a collection edited by Richard T. Hughes called <u>The Primitive Church in the Modern World</u> (1995). After Constantine, he wrote, "<u>Christianitas</u> became the word for the people under Caesar's rule. People outside the empire were heretics... Farther out were the infidels. Only the rare European imagined that any of those people might possibly become Christian, and if they did it could only be as vassals to Rome.... One of the ways that the appeal to the 'way things are'...was baptized [by Constantine] was that the previously pagan cosmological positivism was made into a doctrine of creation. Empire, patriarchy, slavery, and racism are not contingent arrangements that might be challenged, but the nature of things."

In <u>The Politics of Jesus</u>, John called these "contingent arrangements" <u>structures</u>. And while he said we cannot live with them, and cannot live without them: "The church does not attack the powers" that sustain such arrangements and structures; "this Christ has done. The church concentrates upon not being seduced by them. By existing the church demonstrates that their rebellion has been vanquished." (p. 150, 2nd ed.) "[T]he Pauline cosmology of the powers represents an alternative to the dominant ('Thomist') vision of 'natural law' as a more biblical way systematically to relate Christ and creation." (p. 159)

From a Mennonite Police Officer

John saved in his file on law, lawyers, and law schools a short essay by a Canadian police officer, a member of the Toronto Mennonite Church named Morley Lymburner, that appeared in the <u>Mennonite Reporter</u>, April 14, 1986. I have wondered if John planned to some day pull this little essay out and talk to us from it, about training Christians to be lawyers. Mr. Lymburner spoke of three duties he felt in his work--a duty to the individual citizen, a duty to the community, and a duty to God: "This is the tough one. What is this duty? My personal feeling is that the duty of the police officer is that of the good shepherd. He must be ready to protect his flock. He cannot be satisfied that the majority are safe, but must endeavour to watch over all in his charge. He cannot afford to grieve if all his efforts fail; as long as the effort was there, he should be satisfied.

"I can recall as a child my mother speaking to me when I was angry at someone. When vengeance was the strongest in my heart she would tell me that my vengeance was not necessary; if vengeance should come to someone, it would come as surely as the following day. Each person ultimately receives the justice he

On the Possibility of a Christian Law School

deserves. The Lord always sees to it.

"I have carried my mother's words with me on the police force. When I see a criminal set free or found not guilty, those words come back to me. The feeling of vengeance still comes but it is tempered by the thought that at least the effort was there and God knows it as well.

"It is therefore my belief that my duty to God is my duty to his people. I feel that my awareness of this helps me to mete out his justice in his own way. It helps me to realize that justice is not mine to take care of or to enforce. I am but the tool he uses."

Two Sides of the Street

In a draft of a talk I was booked to give the Anglican Chaplaincy at the University of Victoria, I had suggested the image of Christian lawyers, coming from a worshiping community, which might be a Christian law school, as speaking from the church, across the street, to those in the courthouse. John helped me with several terms, and was not charmed by the image:

You state as simple that "modern jurisprudence and legal ethics" makes an idol of the state. Would most of your lawyer colleagues grant that? Is not an argument needed? A lot of them would say, "Not an idol, just the most usable modest messy arbitrator in a setting where there is no clear answer." That person's idol would not be the state but the self.

In your "sides of the street" metaphor the term "parish" may mislead. The parish is a part of the establishment structure where a given church and its clergy have a proprietary claim on and a service obligation to all the people within certain borders and on/to no-one else. The "Baptist" image does not draw such boundaries. People from far away may belong, and neighbors may have no claim. This is not part of your argument; just a leftover fragment of vocabulary.

The word "separate" is easily interpreted as "separatist." The believing community has its own identity and is thus distinguishable, different, from those who deny its <u>raison d'être</u>. But it need not work at shunning or rejecting the others except as those others make unacceptable demands (military service, oath).

It is correct, and important to say, that moral purity is not the point. Identity, being what one says one is, is the point.

Elucidating pacifism is part of my calling, in which people like you support me, but it is inaccurate to suggest that pacifism is centrally or always the witness to the "mainline" church. In 1523-25 the first basis for division was whether the state should structure the church: the Zwinglian position later named "Erastian." The second question was whether dissent and discussion should be repressed by the state. The third was infant baptism. The theme violence/pacifism was around but it was not definitional. It did not divide Zwingli from the protoanabaptists because

he (thought he) was an Erasmian pacifist himself. It became definitional in numerous later settings, but there have still been many times when it was not. Most "Baptists" in [James McClendon's] sense are not pacifist.

If there is to be a modern term it should then be not "pacifism" but "religious liberty." That is harder to discuss because your Anglican audience...thinks they are in favor of it. Their foundational theology however is not. You say the mainline churches accepted the "protection" of the state. Too weak; they affirmed the authority of the state to govern the church.

When Troeltsch said "sect" he was not disdainful. He intended to use the term as a value-free descriptive category, and he gave the early Christians, the medieval and reformation minorities, and the English free church experience such a fair hearing that Karl Holl (Lutheran) condemned him. Numerous sociologists have continued to try to use the term as a value-free ideal type. But the sneer often slips back in, most notably from Stanley's mentor Gustafson.

I don't think the image of the street works for Anglicanism. It is not that courthouse is on one side, church on the other, and something else (liberals would say "the people") actually governs from the street between them. What is above both the church and the courts is the Crown; since 1689, Parliament and the Crown. The courts where lawyers work at troubleshooting, and the church where clergy do cult, and the street department and the post office, are all merely delegated from above.

Being "fuzzy about membership" [in the Erastian church] is too soft a description. "Baptists," too, are fuzzy after the foundational events of a given community have receded by a few generations. What Erastians do is claim jurisdiction over those who do not want it. To this day a Mennonite born in the canton of Basel-Land will be listed, and taxed for support of the state church, unless he goes through a special formality of "withdrawing" from the church which he never joined. Barth's statement is one a Baptist can make.... [Barth, whom I quoted:] "Only this narrow place can offer a vista of the wider space which includes those who are still outside, who are not yet the children of God...but who one day may become and be so." And: "None of us can finally say which others are or are not children of God and therefore brothers and sisters. The idea that one is quite alone in invoking God...is one that the child of God will simply forbid himself, no matter how things may seem around him."

What you say about "active servants going over to the courthouse" could be said too of Roger Williams or William Penn.

The description of Erastianism is modernized. The argument of Erastus and [Richard] Hooker is that it is the will of God that that divinely mandated sovereign (or in the Swiss origins the cantonal senate) which governs all the rest of the civil order should also govern the order of the church; impose creeds, approve bishops and theology professors, pay the clergy.... Once one finds oneself the heir of an Erastian Establishment, then one can [accept those consequences].... Erastus was debating proper church order against the Calvinists, both Presbyterian and Congregationalist. He was not concerned about your problem of the two sides of the street.

"High Church" does in fact designate, in the English experience since Newman, an angle from which to criticize the inclusiveness of Erastianism. More important, though, is that in sociology the "high church" Anglicans who initiated the usage, and the Roman Catholic churches to which the most consistent "high" Anglicans converted, were free churches like the Baptists and the Quakers. They petition Parliament for freedom of speech and assembly and for the right to send their sons to Oxford. They create their own schools when the Erastians won't let them in. They are a tolerated minority. They would rather that Parliament would no longer "sanction and protect" their views by controlling the prayer book. You already notice that they are like the gathered churches in North America; my point is merely that this parallel is more basic. What they differ from Baptists and Quakers about is the criteria for gathering.

You overdo my Socratic question. I would also ask whether a Christian can be a doctor, or a university professor, or a capitalist. My point is that any vocational choice has the burden of proof for a disciple of Jesus. No standard social slot can be a self-evident definition of my obedience to God. By linking this only with law you lay me open to a distortion of the importance of the issues of state and law as worse than something else. I have encouraged Mennonite young people to go into law. I do not see the polar opposition between Mennonite and legal identity which is promoted by the group of Mennonite lawyers with which you once met. The right way to put the question as ethics rather than pastoral care would be "under what conditions can a disciple of Jesus be a lawyer?" or "what kind of lawyer would a disciple of Jesus praise God by being?..." (September 20, 1991)

Community and State

In his unpublished contribution to a jurisprudential symposium held at Georgetown in April, 1989, John said, "(S)ince Aristotle people have been trying, and failing, to speak morally in the name of a community that would be 'everybody.' The state presumes to be that community of everybody for those who live within its borders and to be unaccountable to others. The believer is the person who refuses to acknowledge that claim. What enables that refusal is her/his rootedness in the formative life of a particular community."

John attended a brown-bag colloquium given by Bob Rodes and me, on February 17, 1989, on a theology for Catholic law schools. John did not speak, but he made notes:

Premise--not educating anywhere without knowing why--is earth shattering when measured by real track record of professional promotion.... Shaffer: Few push it to a Niebuhrian crisis. Niebuhrian crisis is a theological construct.... I'm a pacifist. I believe in force--organized resistance.

C. PEDAGOGY

In 1992 I gave a series of lectures on American legal ethics to lawyers and law students in Moscow. I later revised the text of those into a home-made book, which I have used in teaching ethics to American law students in Catholic universities. The last chapter of the book deals with "religious legal ethics" in terms of six propositions:

The first page is a kind of blur; each paragraph, each person, represents the theme in a different way. The Bible as a source of positive law (David Hoffman), the Sermon on the Mount as symbol of idealism (Judge George Sharswood), funeral oratory comparing a good man to Jesus (Judge Thomas Goode Jones), polls about church attendance, all constitute readings on how America is religious. They convey an atmosphere. But the variety tends to confuse rather than clarify what I as a beginning law student would look for in the coming chapter.

Second page brings the [Stephen] Carter agenda; privatizing/secularizing/trivializing. These are very illuminating "anthropology" readings, also contradictory. (Religious sensibility is built in; being inhibited about exposing our religious commitment in the public square is natural; feeling guilty about hiding our faith is natural....) I'm not sure which strand of this complex naturalness is your main point, which will enlighten your reader.

Is a chapter in a legal-ethics book about how to be ethical about being religious, or is it more about how to be religious about being ethical, or mostly about the smaller question (crossover with Carter) of how the legal and the religious dimensions of being human interlock or interact in American law? The attention this page gives to Carter agenda would make me as a beginning student think that the main worry is the spectrum of issues between establishment and secularization. That is a big issue, but is it ethics?

As I move to the six "notions," I again am unsure about the focus.

(1) Saint Atticus [Finch, of <u>To Kill a Mockingbird</u>], your perennial favorite,[32] is great, but the human person being the noblest work of the Creator is an odd way to capsule what Atticus did, what he was "an interesting and more

---

[32] A colleague (not John) once introduced me by saying he had to admire an academic who read a novel and then made a career of it. It was not Atticus Finch, by the way, who said the human person is the noblest work of God. That was James Wilson, an early justice of the federal supreme court, in a tax case.

personal example" of. The Atticus case is an instance:
>--of a lawyer who knows what is the right thing to do;
>--[that] he should do the right thing at all costs;
>--[that] if he didn't, the structure of social obligation would collapse;
>--[that] if he didn't, he could not worship with integrity.

Strong stuff, and reinforcing for the notion of doing the right thing at all cost, but not what a first-year law-school student (or I) would read in your topic sentence. Not a base for substance as to <u>what</u> the right thing is. The <u>content</u> of right lawyering was derived from his profession, not from a view about the place of humankind in creation.

>(2) That God is personlike and benign, which issues in implications:
>>(a) Small choices may be morally important.
>>(b) I should love my neighbors.
>>(c) Much of what the law does contradicts that (b).
>>(d) A benign God may forgive that (c).

A good set of good ideas, not in my mind a single "notion."

>(3) The creator has prescribed a morality:
>>--imitating God; and
>>--loving and serving others.

Here there is clear, double notion, but very formal. As soon as we look closer at the wordings, however, what is needed for a substantial ethic will become less simple.

>>(a) Imitating God by being holy (Lev. 19:2) is in the original setting a matter of cultic or ritual purity, not in the first instance a legal or moral virtue.
>>(b) Imitating God by being perfect (Matt. 5:48) means indiscriminate love, including love of enemy; it is not a cipher or slogan for morality in general.
>>(c) Love neighbor as self is a way to state the degree or the intensiveness or the bindingness of the love, but does not say <u>what</u> is loving to do.
>>(d) The Golden Rule (or its negative formulation by Hillel) is a formal guide for knowing <u>what</u> to do.

Again all of this is great, but much more than a simple notion. Which facet of it will grab a student I cannot guess.

>(4) "Command ethic" adds something to what went before. "Command ethic" is a term in ethical theory (cf. recent book by Richard Mouw). It thus adds a dimension of ethical theory to the very broad "commands" in No. 3. Point No. 4 is more like a single clear notion than the others have been (to me), though the narratives with which you thicken them take more space than the other sections do, and the narratives add the distracting element of a tension between two modes of God's manifestation.

Moral Memoranda From John Howard Yoder

(5) This affirmation ["Conventional (and unconventional) religious organizations are carriers of religious legal ethics"] makes good sense, although it strikes me more as a sociological observation than a religious notion. You are very right in distinguishing between this being the case by default (since the civil order does not do it) and being normatively religious ethics; that would still be one religious community. <u>If and when</u> a civil state <u>imposes</u> secularism, that is also one religious community. Here I revert to my standard polemic according to which...[I disagree with Stephen Carter, who thinks] the 1789 Bill of Rights...is secularized and secularizing and fits into the account of the origins of the trend Carter bewails. But if you with more historical wisdom recognize that the basic Bill of Rights was 1689...a Puritan product, not a secularizing one.

(6) ["A radical example might be instructive."] Obviously valid, but for how many of your readers does the example of a Quaker or Mennonite law student come to life? An honest establishment example might also be instructive: Someone from one of the mainline churches who would live up to her faith would be just as weighty, and just as rare. The Mennonite law student as paradigm does not help with the Stephen Carter problem. It would be more important to help Lynn Buzzard to be less of a Niebuhrian, or to help Richard John Neuhaus to become a less chauvinist American, on grounds of the nonsectarian religious vision they claim to espouse. It would be a harder challenge to write your textbook so as to challenge people from within their own ecology than to refer to the odd hypothesis of a Mennonite lawyer to get people to entertain the notion of non-establishment.

Thank you for continuing to have the patience to provoke and receive my carping commentaries. As the Carter review shows, writing memos to you is an easier way for me to get published than doing work of my own. This reaction is more petty and picky than others because of my concept of the higher standards a textbook has to meet. (January 16, 1995)

Teaching Law in a Mennonite College

I had at one point in my learning theology from John wondered if it might be useful, to the institution and to me, to spend a semester or two teaching at one of the small Mennonite colleges. I sought John's advice. I had hoped to gain insight into to what a Christian legal education might look like:

It would be a privilege to brainstorm with you about why you might be interested in a time as a guest scholar in a small church college, and which college would be most suitable.

I fear you would be seriously disappointed if you would be looking for an institution completely in line with the ideal conception of a tradition of radical discipleship which your benevolent reading of historical types ascribes to my community. Your meeting [with Mennonite lawyers] at Laurelville will already have

On the Possibility of a Christian Law School

shown you how the dynamics of community and professional training have created a group of people who are just as concerned for prestige and promotion as if their grandparents had been Roman Catholic....

For the present it should suffice that I attempt to describe a little more the three largest institutions, which I would think would be the ones the most likely to be open to some kind of guest role for you.

The school in Harrisonburg is the youngest of the three. It was created in the 1920's with the desire to be culturally more conservative and more evangelical than the schools in the Midwest. It has now completely outgrown that definition of its identity, and in fact the process of outgrowing creates some normal dynamics of rebellion and pendulum swings in the other direction. The president who has just taken over this fall is an attorney, the first president not to be called into administration there from the ordained ministry. They have a strong focus on international awareness and service ministries. They also have a strong elementary education program in which the interpenetration between professional and moral values is taken very seriously....

The college at Goshen, Indiana, is the oldest and largest. It has deeper rootage in the renewal of the sixteenth century. It was one of the first schools to build an overseas service experience into the required undergraduate curriculum, and was the first college to have a student exchange program with continental China since the death of Mao. There was a seminary as part of the college but it has moved to Elkhart. And the graduate college does not have especially strong offerings in the field of religion.

The third college is Bethel in North Newton, Kansas.... Its sociology is different because the people it serves migrated into North America more recently, mostly after 1870, mostly from Russia, so that they have a stronger sense of building a complete Christian culture and less of a sense of identity against the world. They have a strong peace studies program with focus on political science dimensions. Their president is a good friend of Mark Hatfield. (August 26, 1987)

John Thinking About Trial Lawyers

Have you ever thought of publishing a casebook of moral problems regarding the defense of evil causes or guilty people? I think you should.

Here is one to add. Four soldiers in Viet Nam, having nothing to do with their time, decided to have an orgy. They seized a very young woman in a hamlet, abused her for several days, and killed her.

Two of the men avowed the crime to authorities and one went to the chaplain. They, however, refused to testify against the ringleader, even though their priest told them it is a mortal sin to refuse. The ringleader however denied it and had an airtight story which resisted all cross-examination. If you are assigned to his defense, do you defend him on the basis of his story and use your cross-examiner's bag of tricks against the persecution witnesses whom you know to be telling the truth?

Does it matter that you think personally that he is a psychopathic killer?

Repercussions: The story was used by Hanoi's representatives in the Paris negotiations to show how U.S. soldiers behaved. A novelized version of the story, Casualty of War, by David Lang, makes the defense lawyer the villain of the novel.

In four separate trials the three other men were given crazily different sentences.

Seriously, a casebook about hard choices on the duty to defend would be a worthwhile service which the Christian lawyers' group could render to the profession, and to the community. (January 15, 1986)

The only section of the acceptance speech of President Bush [the elder] last week which reminded us that four years earlier he had wanted a "kinder, gentler" culture was when he said, "We must sue each other less and care for each other more.... We must put an end to crazy lawsuits."

Is it the case that trial lawyers use any unseemly kind of pressure on the system in order to increase the number of crazy lawsuits?

I have perennially appreciated your frequent attention to other components of ethical sensitivity in the practice of your profession but do not remember having seen you or your colleagues talking about the fundamental concern of social hygiene, that there should be less litigation for certain kinds of offenses, or the larger question of political hygiene, that if this is a moral issue then it would be inappropriate for ethical lawyers to lobby in the interest of that particular malady.

Please let me know when somebody in your school will be dedicating critical attention to this kind of question. (August 25, 1992)

And then there are some short and, I think, relevant observations:

Were I to fill in, I would of course have to clarify the function of "maybe" in ethical discourse. Maybe a Christian cannot be a bishop, or a physician either. (March 6, 1985)[33]

To transpose substance, how be a Chr. If a Lawyer--power-subordin. We too prisoners of polarities, conservatism or liberation, responsibility or escape (anarchism)(egalitarianism). Spirit vs. Institutions: (a) no such problem objectively, either univocal either pole; always more options. (b) newness in NT transforms with new forms, yet with interface to constants. (Notes, August 9, 1989)

[On my pessimism about the niche Christian legal ethics gets in modern

---

[33] John read a draft of my essay, later published as "Maybe a Lawyer Can Be a Servant; If Not..." 27 Texas Tech Law Review 1345 (1996), part of an extensive and ambitious symposium issue entitled "Faith and the Law Symposium."

On the Possibility of a Christian Law School

American law schools:] I think it is a mistake to accept the metaphor of a small room in the attic. You should claim that it is the janitor's closet in the basement, where, even though most people don't go there, and the janitor himself does not clean or decorate it much, it channels the power and heat for the rest of the building.... I don't think there is any tension between large vision and particularity.... Only Hebraic monotheism sees the world whole. (December 29, 1992)

On the way to work this morning I heard on the radio that you have received from the Keck Foundation a lot of money to talk about legal ethics. Congratulations. I hope you are aware that if you hired theologians for this work you could get more people than if you hire lawyers by the hour for it. (January 20, 1993)

I would be grateful for a chance to talk further with you and with [Dean] John Garvey about things that Waco makes us think about. I sense a slight corrupting influence in your connecting such a conversation with...slush funding [available to Shaffer], but I hope that if we watch closely we can avoid letting that corrupt us. (September 8, 1994)

[On an essay of mine, drafted for a journal called Graven Images:] I was unaware of the existence of a periodical devoted to idolatry, and am interested in why they want a text like this [on the argument that biblical forgiveness disrupts legal order].... You seem to me to simplify what you identify as "the legal order," as the only power, or the only reason for not forgiving. This seems to me to leave out other reasons generally appealed to in favor of punishment:

--the psychological demand of the society as a whole and of the families of victims for vengeance or for "closure" (much spoken of whenever a capital decision comes down);

--the metaphysically grounded claim behind the above, studied by [Rene] Girard and [Michel] Foucault, in my paper "You Have It Coming."

Your attention to Jewish sources would be strengthened by the fact that Hannah Arendt stated the functional social imperative of forgiveness in The Human Condition, independent of denominational considerations. [I] critique those who a priori presuppose that only violence works, or that violence is the definition of public order.... (July 29, 1997)

Thank you for the privilege of being able to sit in once again on one of your conversations. The longer I try to figure out "how lawyers think" the more clear it becomes that they think differently and I do not follow. I guess I just was not cut out to be a cultural anthropologist. (March 28, 1996)

John Yoder as Friend, Jurisprude, and Legal Educator

Chapter Four illustrates what a good friend John was. And it illustrates what

Moral Memoranda From John Howard Yoder

I identify as his eclectic, ecumenical, open, and (but) Christocentric approach to ethical discussion:

Legal education was not within John's ordinary academic and ecclesiastical interest, not within his normal concern as a teacher in the theology department, nor within his usual theological focus as a Mennonite preacher and thinker. Law is lethal force; I have thought the way a Christian has to think about the law's claims to order and rationality is the way Reinhold Niebuhr thought about American history–with irony, with a knowing smile. (I tried to explain that thought in "The Irony of Lawyers' Justice in America," 70 Fordham Law Review 1857 [2002].) But when John turned his creative, generous mind to the law he began to see law as a language (I think especially of For the Nations), and he began, I think, to discern in the practice of law and the teaching of it the possibilities for what we Roman Catholics call an apostolate.

Being a lawyer is at best morally problematical. At least we Yoderians think it is, even if John didn't see the moral problems as significantly different from building houses or teaching school. John's tradition has not worked out as much jurisprudence, as, perhaps, Roman Catholics have. (I think of my colleagues John Finnis, Richard Garnett, Teresa Phelps, and Robert E. Rodes, Jr.) I think John Yoder nonetheless had in mind the outlines of an Anabaptist jurisprudence; I discern traces of the project in the material in this chapter. And, at any rate, he would be the first to say that Christians take a sister lawyer where they find her, and from there is able to say that the ethical task is to locate, among the many things lawyers do, what a person might follow Jesus by doing.

Friendship and insight combined for us in the law school at Notre Dame as John demonstrated that he was willing to join in local inquiry and discussion–one of a few theologians on campus who were willing to do that by listening and understanding as well as by giving advice. In particular, for us, John's colleagueship had to do with our university's recurrent spasms of concern over what it calls the Catholic character of the institution and how those spasms played out in the law school. John was, I think, tired of the spasms, but he showed himself willing to take them, in the law school, as seriously as we lawyers did. He was even willing, as you see in this chapter, to turn concern for the Catholic character of the law school into a confrontation and a challenge. He said to us in Northern Indiana, as I heard him say to those who attend the Journal meetings in St. Paul: If you are serious, maybe I can help you out.

Chapter Five

Legal Issues

John Howard Yoder's off-the-cuff discussions of lawyers' issues illustrates as much as anything I know how conceited we lawyers are when we come to think that only lawyers understand the law. That is the theme of this chapter, which gives an array of messages from John that shows both how a sharp, interested person quickly understands whatever it is a lawyer understands about legal questions and of how sharp, interested John Yoder cut through legal formulation. And so–anticipating the examples and cases discussed in this chapter:

- –The grandma-adoption example, a real case in my practice, may be as much about the wisdom of raising a child in the army as it is about the law of fiduciaries for children.
- –Clear argument, to a draft board or a federal judge, for a Roman Catholic conscientious objector, has possibilities one cannot even detect in the statute, the administrative regulations, or the case reports.
- –It is important to keep the moral and political issues in view when lawyers take on cases involving freedom of worship (or, as John liked to think of it, imposed orthodoxy), oppression by tyrants, capital punishment, "welfare reform," and such arcane legal issues as those surrounding practice with the Supplemental Security Income (S.S.I.) rules.
- –There is such a strong connection between the insanity defense and capital punishment that it is not possible to understand one without understanding the other. My distaste for seeing John's interest in Rene Girard, then, declines, as I understand, rather late,

as the connection becomes clearer. (The last time I thought of the connection was when my teacher, the late Professor Anton-Hermann Chroust, associated capital punishment with the primitive pagan practices of sacrificing human beings to the gods. I am left to wonder whether Tony Chroust and John Yoder ever talked to one another about this. Probably not.)

John regularly attended discussions and lectures in the law school. As was true of his attendance in meetings at the annual meetings of the Society of Christian Ethics, though, he steadily took notes, and rarely had anything to say or to ask. Later, then, he raised legal questions he expected a Hoosier lawyer to help him with:

Media reporting about the Cambridge au pair trial provokes questions about the jury system. Is anybody interested in making it more intelligent? Why are they forbidden to take notes? [In Indiana they often do–with the judge's permission.] Is there any way to stop leaving high-income people out of the juries? [Not so far.] Or to reject anti-capital punishment citizens? [Not so far.] (Nov. 5, 1997)

Grandmas, Corporations, Constitutions

I mentioned in John's hearing, in seminar sessions and in lectures, a family situation presented in a group of cases from the Notre Dame Legal Aid Clinic, a student-staffed law office for low-income people in which I have, since 1991, practiced law. The common factor in these cases was that our client was a grandmother who was caring for a small child whose mother had signed up for military service. The military required that someone other than the mother take over care of the child while the mother was in basic military training. The grandmother and the mother had talked about it and had decided to seek adoption of the child by the grandmother -- a permanent and relatively indelible solution that would abolish the mother's legal status as a mother, a result we lawyers were finding morally problematical:[34]

What if the lawyer [in] your scenario were to say that the army is not the best place for the mother to make a life for herself? Is "a child should be with her birth mother" fully true when there is no father? The difficulty when I try to walk along critically with your narrative mode is that there are more parts of the stipulated picture I would want to be free to wonder about. (Nov. 21, 1996)

---

[34] My published discussions of this case are included in "Human Nature and Moral Responsibility in Lawyer-Client Relationships," 40 American Journal of Jurisprudence 1 (1995) and "The Christian Lawyer–An Oxymoron?" America, Nov. 23, 1996, p. 12.

Legal Issues

[Business] institutions are run by managers who do not own the corporation." This could be said more strongly. The notion that corporate shareholders "own" the company is a legal fiction, just as is the notion that "the American people" run the country by voting. The managers in Exxon and the bureaucrats in the Kremlin and the Pentagon do in fact own the country, in the realistic sense that they make the decisions and reap the profits. Share ownership is a scrap of paper. Most shares are voted by fund owners who are managers, too. As I wrote in <u>The Priestly Kingdom</u>, the standard liberal case for democracy needs to be demystified; so does the notion of corporate personality.... (April 20, 1993)

[There is scheduled] a lecture in your courtroom on whether there is a "moral reading" of the constitution.... Title is snazzy, but I don't know what the question means. Is the alternative an immoral reading? An "amoral" one? Who owns the adjective "moral"? Is its being moral validated by criteria from within the constitution or beyond it? I wonder whether the lecturer will question the question or claim to answer it. If there is a moral reading, is there only one? Or could there be several? (Nov. 6, 1997)

The Yoder Perspective on Legal Questions

John was asked to do a comment for the <u>Review of Politics</u>, which is published at Notre Dame. The editor at the time was Professor Donald Kommers, for whom John described the Yoder perspective on talking about legal questions. In a similar vein, he wrote to Professor William T. Buss about his view of legal issues centering around (legal) rights--this in connection with conference papers later published in the <u>Journal of Law and Religion</u>. This part of John's files contains a copy of an op-ed piece by Professor Buss, in an Iowa newspaper, September 2, 1989, entitled "Society unharmed if some choose Christian schools."

My response...[is] an effort to ask what the question looks like from the perspective of the believing community rather than from the more neutral perspective of the civil contract. (Yoder to Kommers, June 27, 1989; copy in Yoder's files)

When a "right" seems so prima facie evident that administrators and legislators find little objection to respecting it, as <u>e.g.</u>, non-taxation of church real estate, or not making Quakers fight, there is not the same occasion for resolving hard cases in the courts. This was one of the things I learned [at a law-and-religion conference, from two law teachers] that I had not taken account of before. It fits with recent experience in the fragility of moral victories soon in the courts <u>(e.g.,</u> restraining the death penalty) without popular support. (Yoder to Buss, August 4, 1989; copy in Yoder's files)

Notes

Moral Memoranda From John Howard Yoder

Liberal democracy founded in human freedom and dignity reaches a point where it can no longer defend its founding principles. (Notes taken during the conference on H. Jefferson Powell's book, <u>The Moral Tradition of American Constitutionalism</u>.)

"...don't have to be fair to a tyrant." JHY then [has] rules for cheating:
    (a) use their rules against [them]
    (b) favored intake [i.e., what cases a lawyer decides to accept]
    (c) get around rules without lying or counseling illegality.

How tell a tyrant? ... Can I do justice in the system? (Notes taken during a discussion of a trial lawyer's practice in criminal defense, July 20, 1993)

"...concept not needed; language rather of duties: Stranger way to speak to the agenda for which "Rights" is the modern profane word: "Law," Covenant, Kingdom--all more adequate.... Ordinary mental reflex: What is one right account, especially since [there is] coercive enforcement...? (Notes taken with reference to a draft I sent him, on the legal profession's rule against a lawyer's vouching for her clients, January 12, 1991)

What Milton was fighting for is freedom of press, assembly. Was not individual nor individualistic. The stake was the glory of God and the Sovereignty of the Word. General intellectual method is doubting...whether Regime is defender or threat.... Talk assumes (or not?) that the government must be satisfied before the question can arise? <u>Ou bien le contraire</u>....

Lawyers say "metaphysical" for "legalistic"....

Skills: Friendship always begins with self-interest. Three codes: friend/crony/immigrant, expanding "family." All three demand a stronger community than the U.S. is.

Humanize even the corporation. Corporation being person is itself a fiction--serving some boss.

Enlightenment made friendship and religion private.... "Choosing models" is enlightenment; always the same. To be open to friendliness to all requires charity as infused virtue. (Undated notes)

On Glendon and Then Carter

You sent me long ago a paper by Mary Ann Glendon on "Structural Free Exercise." I have been reading away at it conscientiously whenever I got free time in that lazyboy, but find it hard to read dense legal texts. I am not competent to determine whether what the author calls "holistic" and "structural" is adequately defined.... (April 20, 1993)

Legal Issues

I respond[35] not so much because I am taken in by your polite suggestion (more the southern gentleman than the Colorado cowboy) that I might add something, as because it gives me an excuse for a break from real work. I'll not try to distinguish between responding to [Stephen] Carter and to you. Obviously the response is in the context of considerable a priori agreement.

One broad observation which applies everywhere, but nowhere in particular: "Religion" is itself a much more fuzzy category than you or your sources or your professional colleagues assume. Cf. 182ff in my Priestly Kingdom. Standard usage assumes that there is one kind of anthropological constant, that everybody deals somehow with the transcendent; the fact that they all do it differently is less basic than the fact that they are all doing the same thing. That is why it makes sense to make that kind of behavior unimportant, because they are all functionally equivalent to one another, all species of the same genus.

If we take Abrahamic monotheism seriously we cannot grant that. The lordship of JHWH or of Jesus is not an alternative to other religions in the genre religio. It is an alternative to other polities and other deities. So I would not take off from what Jews and Christians "call religious...." The point is not that in terms of a set of formal categories some activities are not hobbies because they are religious, but that they are not hobbies because they respond to the command of the true God.

If we are concerned for the right of some people to smoke peyote in Oregon or to kill chickens in Hialeah, maybe they should be compared not to churches but to mental hospitals or lodges....

Carter "relentlessly discounts" the danger that anyone would impose an orthodoxy.... I may share his trust that good law-school liberals will never fall back into obscurantism, but I still don't trust his lack of attentiveness to the intrinsic danger of letting powerbearers use God language. And how about our position unique in the world in not only using but escalating the death penalty for all kinds of offenses?

To reformulate my case against "religion" as all of a kind, or of "assertions based on faith" as properly dealt with all the same way: A religion or a faith which coerces when it can is categorically a different animal from one whose very commitment rejects coercion. This is more than an ethical difference; it is a difference of gods....

About tax exemptions. If there is going to be tax at all, then exemptions from tax are establishment privilege, not a right. I see something wrong with

---

[35]To a draft of my review of Stephen Carter's The Culture of Disbelief: How American Law and Politics Trivialize Religious Devotion (1993). The review was published at 62 University of Cincinnati Law Review 1601 (1994).

establishment in the first place. Once you have it I see nothing wrong in principle with saying that it does not belong to agencies which lobby....

Three kinds of church [gathered, witnessing, and mainline]: The types are helpful but conceptually the order confuses me. The position you call "gathered" is the one into which people from the position you call "witness" retreat when oppressed. In the third or the Nth generation, the rabbis may be content to stay in the ghetto and the Amish on the farm, but from the beginning it was not so. Jewry's assignment in Babylon was to "seek the peace of that city where God has sent you." Withdrawal of "sectarianism" is a subform of witness in a situation of oppression. Sectarians do get killed but witnesses get killed even more; that is why they pull back to being sectarian.

As you move to "Christendom," I see again some gaps I noticed before. The entire church/state discussion, and Carter, and you, are discussing the domestic polity as if that could be done alone. Yet one of the most profoundly anti-Gospel and most profoundly Christendom things people do is war against other peoples. One dimension of the idolatry of patriotism is assuming that this state-nation determines the bounds of our communitarian obligations. The state retains the right to kill its own citizens, but usually tries to do that with due process; the right to kill citizens of other states is far less regulated. The rest of the world is also absent from the Carter agenda with regard to economic rights (N.A.F.T.A., G.A.T.T.) And ecology (Rio). (December 9, 1993)

Notes

No way to adjudicate total clash of systems.

Curve back to "rights." Had moved away to epistemology....

Current phrase, "preferential option for poor": language clarity–"options," "poor," "widow/orphan/alien"–"no shot," "no advocate." I.e., not from the center of system but from its failures. Points to a difference reaching further: Catholic vision optimistic [about] human nature...good society from top down...vox populi. Protestant...basically suspicious ("case for democracy").

From same perspective another difference: Arising of "religious liberty" issue.... For centuries persons talking about authentic faith said it couldn't be forced and yet didn't challenge repression of heretics. The way to discover religious liberty is to BE the heretic. I.e., the disobedience comes first.... The prior question is where get the "place to stand" to come to dissent: Historical practical events. Can't come from common (reason)(nature). (August 2, 1989)

John had a running disagreement with Professor Harold Berman, who has been for decades the most prominent of a small cadre of American "law and religion" scholars. Berman writes from a perspective John would have called "Constantinian."

Two swords is not two realms. The visible church questions orders for good life.... B. overdoses pessimism--positivism; trust the ruler; 1525 reversal; peasants' cause just....

Limits of obedience: Luther, too.... First Amendment only because of factual pluralism.... Francis and heresy: Branches of Franciscan movement had mission of converting heretics.

Church was not a community but a State....

I am probably not as optimistic as you about the practical advantages of having both feet in one discipline.[36] (March 27, 1989)

Some Public Legal Issues

[I sent John a reprint of an article on "religious outlaws," by Professor Barbara Bezdek, with a short note written on the cover.]

There is Shafferian irony in your note,"You may have missed this," when it is common knowledge that the world of law reviews is by nature inaccessible to the lay person. I had not been looking for it.

As with the death penalty, I am interested to know how the "Catholic character" of legal education in our law school includes some component of bias in favor of the underdog on the grounds of denominational identity.

I appreciate the way the author distinguishes the categories of "civil disobedience," "civil initiative," and the Nuremberg appeals.

I also was educated by the exposition of the way in which the courts' denial of evidence [was] on the grounds that dissent from present policy is not relevant.... To the layman this is a breach of the separation of powers (in that the judicial branch does not accept challenges to the administrative), as well as a denigration of religion. (March 4, 1996)

John and I were both involved, professionally and personally, in the issue of "selective" conscientious objection. My remark to John, speaking as a lawyer, representing clients who sought C.O. status from a religious and philosophical stance that says some wars are immoral and some are not, was that I hoped to get my selective-objector early, so that I could train him to make a claim that did not admit a selection among wars, since legal conscientious-objection protection is limited to those who object to all wars. The idea was, during the Viet Nam War, announced by the folk singer Joan Baez, who suggested such responses to draft boards as: "This (Viet Nam) is the only war I know; I cannot know what I would have done in 1941." John's thought on the point seemed to me not to recognize that the law of conscientious objection in the United States rests on legislative grace, not on the

---

[36]A reference to the modest first chapter in Mary's and my book <u>American Lawyers and Their Communities</u> (1991).

federal constitution, and that judges try to follow precedent.

My argument [is] about the way conscientious objection is seldom litigated as an "exemption"--because it is not usually respected by legislation--[and] my claim [is] that selective objection, if properly argued, as a prima facie valid claim, would not seem to be set aside by saying that sometimes earlier judges did not include conscientious objection in [the constitutional protection] of free exercise [of religion]. The question would seem to me as a non-lawyer to be about what is the proper way to litigate it. (Yoder to Shaffer, undated)

On Going to Church

I was struck by a newspaper column--rather more than John was, as it turned out--by a journalist who wrote to explain why it is important to him to attend services in his Episcopal parish:

What does [he] go [there] to get? Consolation? Reassurance that there is another dimension to life? You had already discerned that it does not show in how he articulates political opinions or in what those opinions are. (April 20, 1993)

On Welfare Litigation

Public radio has been telling us about the vices of central government and the virtues of your profession.

As they tell it, the "reform" of welfare has meant a peremptory removal of one whole category of families with handicapped children from the roles entitled to receive S.S.I. support for their care.

The removal was rapid, without clear warning, on a guilty-until-proven-innocent basis. Appeal was possible but had to be done by the parents at their own initiative with a very short time window.

The American Bar Association has set up special network for pro-bono counseling. The appeals which have been processed have thus far restored 60 per cent, which would seem to indicate that the presumption of not being qualified was unfair.

I assume there is some selfish interest which led the A.B.A. to help with this with such alacrity. Still it would seem to be commendable. (November 21, 1997)

Public radio, which a month ago reported that the A.B.A. was doing a lot of pro bono work in favor of handicapped people who had their S.S.I. benefits taken away unfairly, now says that 45,000 cases (a third of those who lost benefits) will be reviewed. Makes me wonder what were the forces and/or motivations within the social security bureaucracy which would have been so strongly anti-client in downsizing the welfare system. (December 18, 1997)

Legal Issues

The Insanity Defense

Again needing guidance to understand your world.

What is the legal and cultural background for the insanity defense? If ignorance of the law is no excuse why is not knowing that what one was doing was wrong? Now Kaczinski's defense is going to plead that while very intelligent he has another kind of disorder. Sounds a little like "superior orders" in Nuremberg.

"Forgive them for they know not what they do" is Jesus, but only in Matthew (23:34), and not in all the manuscripts. Whom does "they know not" cover? What did they not know? Why is that an excuse?

Martyr Stephen (Acts 7:60) had no such qualification. Forgiveness in Matt. 18:15ff is contingent on "hearing" but not on ignorance. So the closer I try to look, the less clear it is why the judicial system has been so sure about exculpation through ignorance or reduced capacity.

Elsewhere in the N.T. what illuminates the choice to forgive is not the state of mind of the culprit but that of the one offended: Forgive him as God has forgiven you.

These questions become important in new ways as "truth commissions" or "reconciliation commissions" in newly legitimate states are authorized to forgive. Sometimes "remorse" is cited as grounds for leniency by the courts or for clemency by a governor. In South Africa a requirement is that the motivation for the atrocity had to be political.

My interest is not in how the M'Naughten rules[37] are stated or how they are applied so much as in why it seems in the first place, in the English common law system, that intent should make a difference for guilt and therefore also for forgiveness. Is there some standard reading on the cultural roots of the incompetency plea?

At the dedication of a memorial at Auschwitz, Eli Wiesel dramatically invoked God not to forgive, because only the victim can ask that of God (or only the victim can herself/himself forgive). There are new theological books on forgiveness, three by friends of mine. I sense such a proliferation of meanings that I wonder about trying to spread them on a typology. Certainly one of the places to look must be the origins of the incompetence or insanity plea...

---

[37]"McNaughten rules (mik-nawt-en).... The doctrine that a person is not criminally responsible for an act when a mental disability prevented the person from knowing either (1) the nature and quality of the act, or (2) whether the act was right or wrong. The federal courts and most states have adopted this test in some form." Black's Law Dictionary 994 (7th ed. 1999). The rules were first announced in a case in the House of Lords in 1843.

Moral Memoranda From John Howard Yoder

In the light of the unclarity about <u>why</u> insanity should exculpate I understand the movement being reported to replace "not guilty by reason of insanity" with "guilty but insane." But the latter still decreases the level of punishment. (November 22, 1997)

Thank you for continuing to send material on the insanity defense and its counterparts. I am curious because of cross-references to other matters:

Does it relate to "Father, forgive them because they know not what they do"? I.e., how is liability or forgivability conditioned on being unwitting? Compare to the present South African truth and reconciliation process, where a condition for amnesty is that the atrocity was politically motivated.

I do not understand what was the reason in the first place for considering insanity as a defense, in the cultural/anthropological setting of the time. That depends of course on the cultural/anthropological basis for punishment as such.

Speaking of the social role of punishment: Public radio interviewed a mother of children killed in the Oklahoma City bombing who said that she thought Terry Nichols would be found guilty and "then we can go on." <u>I.e.</u> the reason for killing people [with capital punishment] is a need <u>located within the persons of the relatives of the victims</u>? That strikes me as an anthropological observation which we do not take seriously enough. (December 18, 1997)

On Citizenship

It is epistemologically backward to put the question thus: "The state is defined as xxx; can a Christian have to do with it?" Proper epistemology would say: "The Kingdom of God is like....; what does that tell me to share with my neighbor, who has not joined me in following Jesus, but whose human dignity I am pledged to affirm, in our common life." Often there will be things to do that are of higher priority for the disciple to do than running the jails; but if so the reason for that is the stewardship of creativity, not a legalism which writes off certain territories. (September 20, 1991)

On Arguing From the Past (a Frequent Practice Among Lawyers)

In his paper "The Ambivalence of the Appeal to the Fathers," John argued that biblical arguments were preferable to arguments quoting eminent or memorable forebears--and this even though "the recovery of history is indispensable.... The retrieval of history is christologically mandated":

Finally, though, it is a mistake for radical reformers to "concentrate on our origins." Better "to hang loose, as they did, from defined institutional positions, even the right ones, affirming the link with the New Testament and <u>with all the faithful through the centuries</u>, yet without privileging one set of founders."

Legal Issues

"(T)oday's renewal agenda (sexism, power abuse, genocide, ecology) calls for a kind of radicality for which the restructuring of church life and personal discipleship, though necessary, is insufficient." (John cited Hebrews 13:13ff:) "Therefore let us go forth to him outside the camp, bearing abuse for him. For here we have no lasting city, but we seek the city which is to come." (R.S.V.)

Law Students Respond

My students in jurisprudence read John's paper "Ethics and Eschatology." (See Chapter Three.) I sent John the papers they wrote, reflecting on what I gave them of Yoder. Two–one an Oklahoma Methodist and one an Italian Catholic–joined together to comment on what John wrote about criminal punishment: "We came to the conclusion that people can be deserving of punishment, that punishment can be correctly decided and implemented, and that others can be comfortable with the acceptance of this punishment. But the fact remains, deserving or not, some other human being has had to undergo an undesirable experience, and there is a great difference, from a Christian perspective, (between) accepting this and rejoicing in it. We feel that Christian principles stress that we should strive toward not getting pleasure from other people's pain. When we looked back on those times that we had rejoiced at others' misfortune, we did not feel that we were better for the experience; rather, we felt petty and vindictive. In our minds one of the Christian goals is to be governed by compassion rather than (by) vengeance."

<u>For the Nations</u> As Jurisprudence

I conclude this chapter with a few paragraphs of my review of John's <u>For the Nations</u>, which was published in the <u>Legal Studies Journal</u> in 1998. This book of John's is not only his late word on legal issues, but also, I think, his clearest. Page references are to John's book.

Is this politics? And then, if it is politics, is it also jurisprudence? (Which would be to set aside for the moment whether, as the Critical Legal Studies movement taught us, all law is politics.) Yoder argued, from Indiana and Kentucky to Europe, from Latin America to South Africa, that <u>all</u> of theology is politics: **"How you see the adversary and the wider human community is the very substance of politics. Love of the enemy and respect for the out-group is not politically <u>popular</u>, but it is politically relevant and politically right." (193) It is politics replacing "...the legacy of 'Christendom' according to which the authority to speak of the public good belonged to the king, who had that role by divine right and graciously shared some of it with his noble cousins of the aristocracy, and some of it with his noble cousins in the clergy. That was the prevailing system from the fourth century to the nineteenth, although other perspectives began to break through the crust** beginning in the fifteenth." (19) It is politics replacing democratic liberalism (which is, when you trace through the last quotation, and make some minor substitutions, not all that different from the politics of Christendom).

Speaking to faculty and students in the Roman Catholic seminary in Baltimore, in 1994, Yoder said: "The vision of things I have been invited to present...is at home in no one semantic world, in no one social world." (51) Speaking in a world where his vision of things was closer to being at home, at his own Goshen College, in Indiana, three decades earlier, he reminded those in the believers church that trust in processes of discernment is more important than taking positions: "Part of what it means to be the believers church is to believe that there are answers that we don't have yet." (161) Writing for the World Council of Churches in 1980, he said, "'Sign,' rather than 'instrument,' describes more properly how our words and deeds 'work.'" (240)....

Yoder's project was, as he said, political, and, I think, jurisprudential; and...his project was politics and jurisprudence because it was (not based on or rooted in, but was) the community of faith. He refused to define the church as "...an aggregation of loose individuals each trying by himself to be Christian in his place." (114) He refused to define it as an administrative structure; on the contrary, the church is, he said, "a congregation, a rediscovery, a way to overcome Constantinianism as it protects against the special distortions of seeking authority for a clerical elite." (114)

The church is "the body of persons gathered around the name of Jesus Christ." (115) "[T]he church is the one society in which the terms of membership-- namely, the confession of faith and cross-bearing obedience to Jesus Christ--would, to the extent to which it is honored, make people less rather than more selfish." (115) Because people in the church are made less selfish, the church as politics (and as jurisprudence) is "alternative leverage on the social order" (148), so that its very believing is an "alternative stance in the social order." (148)

Politics (Jurisprudence) and Biblical Process

When Yoder wrote this way, he recognized that a community of faith <u>could</u> function politically by relying on its biblical processes. Given that understanding, he could (and did) talk about communities from Abel's to Abraham's to Jesus's: "For these people, to be <u>believing</u> meant acting in obedience despite the lack of evidence that obedience would 'work.'" (149) What these biblical models of the political (and legal) did was "to hope, to love, on grounds that the world cannot take away." (150) The biblical processes <u>are</u> politics.

Several of the chapters in <u>For the Nations</u> were talks directed to communities of "sectarian" Christians. To them, and when he sought with mainline Christians to clarify the witness of the believers church, he said: "Many hopeful things are also possible things to do. Thus when I say we are freed from the pessimism of system-immanent analysis, that does not mean that we don't care about mechanisms and social analysis, political (legal?) analysis, and calculation of results. It means that that caring is held within a wider trust." (151) "[T]he imagery of the hope that makes no sense but keeps us obeying even when we don't see the victory behind it is still, for this theme, the clearest way to live in a biblical cosmology." (153)

Some of Yoder's description of the believers church was a matter of what has come to be called "lifestyle." In law, in politics, in professional life, members of the believing community will manifest a certain "commonality of style," he said, division of labor, a capacity to be effective that depends on "having a community in the stance of opposition"--and "it is worth reminding ourselves that the value of the believers church approach to problems is partly that it offers, practically, better ways to do things." (154) Without being in the mainstream, without being among those who "take responsibility for managing the culture." (155)

And that, of course, requires "an ongoing critique relative to our own identity." (157) I thought when I read that of a story I heard, years ago, from a scholar whose research had been among the Amish of Lancaster County, Pennsylvania. Someone had noticed that those farmers--who have for centuries powered their machinery with horses and taken their families to town in buggies--had started using a corn sheller powered by a gasoline engine. They put the sheller on a wagon drawn by horses, took it to the field, and cranked it up to shell corn. The person who noticed this wondered if using a corn sheller was consistent with Anabaptist doctrine on machinery. The answer he got was that the Amish do not have a doctrine on machinery; they have a way of life; and they decide, when a farming device comes to their attention, whether the device will weaken their way of life. They decided, in the case put, that a gasoline powered corn sheller, operated a good space away from the house, would not....

The Centrality of Pacifism

Finally, a word from Yoder on the difference between being violent and being aggressive:

The obituary [Peter] Steinfels wrote (in the New York Times) led with Yoder's pacifism, and much of Yoder's significance as a prophet and teacher will (whether it should or not) boil down to his teaching on lethal violence. I hope, within that inevitability, that those who learn from Yoder will understand how broad and how politically radical a theology of nonviolence is and can become. I hope unbelievers and Jews and those in the mainline church will not dismiss Yoder's politics and jurisprudence by deciding to tolerate it.

Yoder said his social ethics, his politics, his jurisprudence "has something

to do with whether we are able to talk back to the authorities, whether we have the psychic wherewithal to see our world the way the New Testament saw its world." This has involved concern, among aggressive pacifists, for the fact that modern liberal democracy does not imprison, torture, and kill Anabaptists, as Catholic Christendom and the Christians of the Reformation did. It has to do even with the fact that pacifists, particularly "peace church" pacifists in modern America, don't have to <u>suffer</u> for their faith as much as their forebears did.

"It has to do with whether the gratitude we feel because we have been taken in by authorities who are good to us because we're good to them--we pay our rent, we don't revolt--whether that gratitude has destroyed our capacity to see the monstrosity of rampant nationalism for what it is...the ease with which we have fallen into a simplification of the problem in the past, assuming that the relation of church to world is a stable polarity. The world's out there, we are over here, we are polarized, but we are also settled into that differentness, so that we have to let the world go its way while we go our way." (158)

The thing for aggressive pacifists is to hold on to "apocalyptic tension" with the world, never to say that what the world is is all right just because we're different. (159) "Being 'sectarian' may free us from despair at our failure to get things done fast, but it won't free us from responsibility." (159) "To hope and solidarity let us add the accountability that means that we won't go off alone." (160)

Epilogue

On Learning About Law from John Howard Yoder

In 1985, in an issue of the <u>Christian Legal Society Quarterly</u>, I wrote a short review of John's <u>The Priestly Kingdom</u>. Even more than <u>The Politics of Jesus</u>, that book has given me and my students an orientation to a jurisprudence and a legal ethic that I think of as based on John's theology:

At first Yoder's religious ethics seem commonplace to Jews and Christians: **"What is of interest is far less the question of how ethical obligation is to be formulated and far more the question of whether or not one is going to obey the Lord who commands."** (109) And then you get to thinking about it and reading more, and you realize that our noble commitments are what corrupt us–especially the commitments that come from our being "a Christian nation," or "a church for all people," or from a profession that uses law to make things better. We look at a profound and stubbornly cryptic Yoder sentence such as, **"A repentant view of history is more creative than an eulogistic one"** (95), and we wonder (some of my students who read <u>The Priestly Kingdom</u> have wondered, I think) whether the routine, the prosperity, and the power in our lives as church people and as lawyers might have put a wall between us and the prophets God sends to us.

Yoder demands–demands–that he be considered in those terms. He resents being spoken of as a consultant from the "sectarian" or Anabaptist, or peace church, or free church tradition. He is often consulted and is always generous in response: but it is clear in these essays that he wants to be heard as a Christian speaking in the church and to the church, and not some kind of ecumenical delegate: **"Let it be recalled that (contrary to a common misinterpretation) the initial intention of the** 'sectarian' communities which in the course of Western history have renewed a minority ethic has not been to be sects. Division was not their purpose. They have called upon all Christians to return to the ethic to which they themselves were called." (85)

"There was...one time when the ethical orientation referred to here as the free church view was dominant among Christians.... This was the church of the first three centuries. Here there were division and divergencies among Christians, but with regard to the morality of violence, the oath, wealth, and high imperial office, the views in ancient literature were largely those which were renewed by Anabaptists and Quakers.... There is no moral guidance that is not of the gospel.... There is no gospel which does not have the form of Torah, i.e., of necessarily calling for and enabling specific commitment in the style of moral relations." (112-113)

Approaching "the Majority Tradition" in Friendship

Yoder comes as a critic of "the majority tradition"–of all of us who grew up thinking that just as cleanliness was next to godliness, so America was God's new Israel. But he also comes in a spirit of fraternal correction; he comes as a brother, inflexible in his own calm way but always listening. (I hear his voice in this book in both ways, as I and my students have in both ways heard it in person.) He does not come insisting on his theology; he comes inviting us to read the Bible with him. And in his mind is God's promise to be with the church–forever: **"We should feel guilty, not when we need to be corrected but when we claim to bypass that need, as if our link to our origins were already in our own hands." (70)**

Yoder was a vocal member of the Mennonite community in Northern Indiana (long associated with Goshen Bible Seminary), and also was a professor of theology at Notre Dame University. His previous books include treatments of pacifism, of the theology of Karl Barth, of ethics, and biblical exegesis. The best known of these, The Politics of Jesus...is an analysis of Luke's gospel that I found–as I find much of this new book–uniquely compelling. The descriptive phrase that Yoder's position deserves, above all others, is Radical Reformation. All of his work is filled with a forthright determination to get the mud and the hard little stones out of the way, to lay bare the roots. He wants us to see the roots and remember who we are.

The two arguments that were most important to him are free choice and non-violence. Anabaptism's label identifies it as insisting on free membership (and therefore the baptism of adults). Its peculiar place in American ecclesiology has been its insistence on peaceful witness. But it is not the case, he says, that the radical reformer shuns civic responsibility or denies the gospel's insistence that Christian witness speak to all people:

"What matters to the radical reformation position is not its radicality but

Epilogue

its Lord. In situations where that appeal to the normativeness of Jesus does not trigger defensive expulsions, the free church has no commitment to schism or to extremism." (88)

"We report an event that occurred in our listeners' own world and ask them to respond to it. What could be more universal than that?" (59)

"The exercise of civil power need not be boiled down by definition to the wielding of the sword. A sectarian ethic can, when it has a chance, govern an American colony (William Penn) or can exercise major institution-building pressure and creativity (Gandhi, King, Dolci). Thus to argue that for believers to derive their ethic from Jesus demands that they withdraw from society is...an argument which follows neither from empirical experience nor from the content of the gospel message, but from the hermeneutic aprioris of the majority traditions." (115-116)

In fact, though, the free church tradition has characteristically been in a minority–and persecuted–position. This has given it a certain perspective, a view not so much from the bottom of the pile as from a place that seems powerless. That perspective (one could call it peaceful) gives Yoder insights that are denied to those of us who write from one of the world's command posts. He notices, for example, that his tradition may appear to Calvinists, Catholics, and Lutherans to be passive in the face of social evil. But: "One of the differences between being powerful and powerless is that one has thought more about the fact that there are evils one cannot prevent." (101)

Disestablishment (of the church), he says, is "not simply an accidental trait but an affirmative definition." (105) If you press Yoder on the point, he is likely to talk about the powerlessness of Jesus and to scoff at the mainline church's claiming responsibility and guilt for what our "Christian nation" does: "Nor can we bring justification like that of Reinhold Niebuhr, to the effect that any growing community will have to dilute its morality a little in order to take charge of a society for the good of that society." (78)

An Assessment

Those are the categories. Beyond them, what seems most significant for me, in talking about the law I learned from John Yoder, is that he was my friend.

I mean more than that he was a good colleague, although he was. John was regular and faithful in his university scholarship. You could depend on his being willing to join in, to contribute in his terse and even cryptic way (a style of discourse I finally came to smile about), to do his job well and faithfully. I would guess that he thought about this less as his job, though, and more as a civic expression of love of neighbor and a local expression of his willingness to contribute to what Catholics call the common good. He did not, though, set much store by academic discourse as a way of discerning truth. Being an exemplar colleague is not what I mean when I say he was my friend. I suppose, though, since we shared a campus, it was part of his friendship for me.

Nor do I mean social and congregational friendship. John and his family maintained their congregational life in Elkhart and Goshen, not at Notre Dame. And, aside from his and Mrs. Yoder's joining in an occasional gathering on campus, I have no insight into their social life.

What I mean mostly by saying he was my friend, and that his friendship was important to me, is that he responded generously and without condescension when I, a Hoosier lawyer across campus, self-taught (if taught at all) in theology, turned to him for help, he gave it to me as one who sought, in friendship, to collaborate in the good. He helped so that I did not feel my preliminary thoughts (however mistaken) were not worth having. That is a rare and special thing among those who try to work across disciplinary lines in the scholarly life. Many times, as the contents of this collection demonstrate, he kept me going. That is what you might hope to get from a friend.

For one thing, you pick up ways of thinking from someone you admire. And if I haven't changed my own ways of thinking as much as I would like, because of him, I have learned to notice what they might become.

He was the most <u>eclectic</u> believer I ever met. He thought of himself as a resident alien in American Roman Catholic culture, but he entered it generously, willing always to learn, and then, remarkably, to teach us Catholics about the implications of our commitments. I doubt that he ever, for a moment, found just-war theory useful for himself or his Mennonite Church. But if you were to ask, during, say, the Gulf War, who at Notre Dame was expert on just-war theory, the informed answer would have been: John Howard Yoder.

He once told me he was the only member of the Notre Dame theology faculty who at that time taught Catholic Social Thought.

He was willing to tell us in the law school what a Christian law school should be doing, and he put that advice in specifically Catholic terms.

At Washington and Lee, John accused James Gustafson's "theocentric ethics" of having abandoned Gustafson's Reform Church tradition. On a later visit to Lexington, John preached at Sunday services in R.E. Lee Memorial Episcopal Church. He wore his impressive academic regalia from Basel. And he of course preached very well.

His eclecticism explains, I think, his wariness over the identifier "sectarian." That word is used mostly by Christian theologians to dismiss other Christians without listening to them (aimed as I suppose "conservative," "Christian Right," or "Fundamentalist," are aimed, although aimed in the opposite direction). John tended to insist on not being dismissed; witness his tenacious resort to his "questions" about narrative theology. He was willing to accept "sectarian" if his interlocutor

Epilogue

would agree that it meant "pacifist," did not mean John was ducking (any or all) intellectual engagements, and especially if it did not mean that everybody supposed John did not seek the peace of the city.

He preferred, he said, to enter an argument obliquely. He liked to bypass the question on the table and talk about other questions. He disliked what he called "Punctualism." (This, when you think about it, is part of the "hermeneutics of peoplehood," which is more about discernment than about debate.) And so, in responding to my Grandma-adoption dilemma, he did not talk about the rights of mothers versus grandmothers, but about putting mothers in the Army. When I raised this dilemma with a Presbyterian Sunday School class, I thought about John: Some present wanted to talk not about adoption rights, but about the parties' personal commitments to the Lord. Similar hermeneutics, I think. The practice, John said, **"answers differently a question being asked so...that it draws attention to other questions."**

These qualities in John were not contrariness. He was willing to argue in terms being used, to cooperate with the "more normal vehicles of political discourse," to translate into whatever language would work. His oblique style was in and of discernment (even if it was often a surprise to those accustomed to tighter notions about relevance). I suppose he might speak about that as he spoke about surprises in scripture: **"My hope is that the oddity of the literature of the seers may continue to shake or to shock us into the recognition that the limits our moral systems impose on our moral possibilities need not be the last word."**

And, of course, behind these habits and–pardon the word, John–tactics, there dwelt a certainty, a comfort that what he thought, what he knew from being a biblical Christian, was for everybody: **"We report an event in our listeners' own world and ask them to respond to it. What could be more universal than that?"**

Lessons

There are a few focal lessons that deserve note, because they were seminal for my own middle-aged thinking and in my attempts to formulate and dispense a theological legal ethic to my students and fellow lawyers:

What the law is, for example. John was a lot better on the law than I, in my pride, conceded to him at the times he helped me. He had been instrumental, for example, in setting up the test case that Bill Ball (a Notre Dame law alumnus) argued and won in the federal supreme court: Wisconsin v. Yoder (no kin). That decision remains a sort of legal bulwark protecting the church in the United States from American public education.

He was far more prescient than I was about the disaster in Waco, Texas. Where I thought the immediate legal aftermath there was going to be confined to the criminal trials of Waco survivors, John saw it as the deeper issue that became the investigation of a special prosecutor and the subject of congressional hearings--in prolonged civil litigation, brought in the federal courts, by those who suffered and survived the attacks of the Federal Bureau of Investigation. John looked for those sorts of legal reaction, and they finally came. We will, I hope, talk about them when next we meet.

He was insightful in his argument with me that the status of <u>selective</u> conscientious objectors (those who follow just-war theory into their consciences) should rest on constitutional civil liberty and not on congressional grace. I was right, of course, as was Joan Baez–and we both had some success–in choosing evasive tactics when we represented these objectors before draft boards and judges. But John was right in principle and in clear-sighted understanding of what Christian witness should be in such a case. At least one judge--a federal trial judge in San Francisco, as I recall--agreed with John about the federal constitution.

He was often right on the law, less often right, though, <u>about lawyers</u>. When it came to lawyers (for all of his gentle understanding of this one Hoosier lawyer), he was capable even of what for him was rare indeed--the cheap shot:

--When the American Bar Association called for lawyers to volunteer (without pay) to represent children stricken from the Supplemental Security Income rolls in 1997, John said he assumed there was "some selfish interest" involved.

--When he pondered with me the significance of the legal career and the theology of the late Episcopalian lawyer, William Stringfellow, John thought Stringfellow avoided the moral stress that would have been involved had Stringfellow faced membership in his "guild" as a vocational crisis. I did not, and do not, think so. Stringfellow's determination to be a "biblical person working in the law" remains significant for me and, I hope, for my students. It is a case, to use a phrase of John's in another context, a matter of "caring within a wider trust."

--John got me invited to meet with an organized group of North American Mennonite lawyers, a meeting in which I taught a little, learned a lot, and made lasting friendships. Before and after that meeting, though, John seemed to not understand those lawyers. Their pondering their faith and their work was, I think, an instance of their following <u>his</u> leadership, "to let truth govern our own choice of whether to be, in our turn, tyrants claiming to be benefactors." Maybe, I thought, as I made new friends among those lawyers, it is possible for lawyers to focus on the tiny deeds John talked about, as if they were mothers with children in school, craftsmen who do their work well, drivers who stay on their own side of the road, police officers who hold their fire.

I confess to having in mind, as I sit down to write this, a complaint John Yoder did not provoke--what I hear about lawyers in America as the national politicians are going to and fro on whether patients should be able to file lawsuits against their health maintenance organizations. The press provokes me into defense of my "guild" as it assumes that all actors in this modern drama are legitimate when

Epilogue

they seek to make a living from what they do--doctors, managers, bureaucrats, congressional people--all <u>except</u> lawyers, who are only in the game to make money at it, which, when lawyer income is in focus, seems always to mean gouging.

The issue I have with John about lawyers is probably better considered under the broader Christian ethic I learned from him. ("Applied ethics," as I learned from Alasdair MacIntyre, is almost always a mistake.) And that is finally an issue about communities capable of discerning the truth--about "the hermeneutics of peoplehood"--than it is about the particular moral questions lawyers debate among themselves and do not submit to their sisters and brothers in the Lord.

It is tempting (as John taught me to understand) to affirm integrity at the cost of witness. That affirmation describes "professionalism." (It is what Stringfellow resisted, by the way.) That is why it is so hard for a lawyer, as a lawyer, to find a place to say that "servanthood, enemy love, and forgiveness would be a better way to run a university, a town...a factory," or a law practice. John said we lawyers are afraid to try that, because we fear failure. I suspect it is because those ways of living are just not professional. The issue becomes clearer, either way: It is eschatological. Jesus is Lord. The battle has been won. Legal order to the contrary notwithstanding.

I came slowly, as Yoder's student, to believe that being able to see lawyers' issues that way depends on more than reading good books and talking to good lawyers: It depends on a <u>discerning community</u>, on the processes John described, from scripture, in "The Hermeneutics of Peoplehood," on a place, a community, **"where the redeemed individual and the social structure are both present, namely, in the Christian community as a visible body."** As he wrote, **"The primary social structure [with] which the gospel works to change other structures is that of the Christian community."** This is true of our political issues (what the government ought to do), and of our jurisprudential issues (what the law ought to do), and of "personal" moral issues that most of us who practice law have learned to ponder all alone.

John meant the community as a normative resource, as a place to figure out what to do. More fundamentally, though, he identified the church as epistemology--as a place from which to see what is going on (H. Richard Niebuhr's first ethics question) as well as what God is doing in the world (his second). (In <u>The Responsible Self</u>, Niebuhr reformulated these questions as, "To whom am I responsible? And in what community?")

The discerning community is reliable, then, in ways not available to the civil society or the state. Which means that the discerning community and those (lawyers) it advises are free to experiment, to be creative, <u>precisely because they can afford to be right</u>. We can, from such a communal base, experiment, test, confirm, update, and apply understanding. **"The church is both the paradigm and the instrument for the political presence of the gospel."** Thinking like that is what happens when a Hoosier lawyer who is also a mainline-Baptist-turned-Roman-

Catholic gets a bit of an Anabaptist angle on things. It is how I began to understand that John was talking not only about the politics of Jesus, but also about the jurisprudence of Jesus. And from there one might attempt the greatest oxymoron of them all--the legal ethics of Jesus.

The church, John said, can discern better in these (epistemological and normative) ways, because it does not seek power. If that non-seeking should happen among Christians (it rarely does among Baptists and Catholics), then, in the odd way John liked to talk about power, it is a form of servanthood that finds itself in a position of power, in possession of a way to make things happen. What is novel then is that this power--lawyer's power, say--turns **"from coercion to persuasion, from self-righteousness to service."**

I was never sure how much John was willing to admit that a lot of living that way takes place in law offices; we could agree that a lot more could. My complaint under the heading of moral discernment, in the church, on moral questions in the practice of law, is more against the church than against my fellow lawyers. If change of the sort John wrote about were to sink in in mainline Christian congregations, the Radical Reformation would have come home.

I have experimented a bit--not enough, but a bit--with this jurisprudence, in law practice, in law teaching, and in the church. Not enough experimentation to change very much (who knows?), but enough for me to see some of the implications:

--The practice of law from the church carries with it a certain "commonality of style," as John put it. A certain division of labor in the community (and, with that, trust in the competence of those who do other things--dependence on them). It carries with it a lot of listening. John's basic scriptural rules for processes of discernment in the church were that everyone gets to talk, and everyone listens.

--It carries with it the understanding that, as the discerning community is perceived as standing for something (we American Catholics stack that under "Catholic Social Teaching" and then ignore it), **it will become a "community in the stance of opposition." It will suggest "a better way to do things." It will (for the most part) offer its participation in "responsibility for managing the culture," even when it knows it will not be taken up on the offer. "Reality is multi-dimensional," John said.**

--What is finally important for the discerning community is its own trust in its own processes of discernment, even when it finds that there are answers it cannot discern: **"Part of what it means to be a believers church is to believe that there are answers that we don't have yet."**

--Where answers are discerned, they are provisional. John and I used to talk about the Rabbis and about the scholarship of our sometime colleague Roger Brooks; the Rabbis insisted that their authoritative answers to moral questions were tentative; they preserved for the future the answers they had rejected; John pointed out that they were lawyers.

Epilogue

--No one is excluded from this "hermeneutical circle." John was wary of the traditional habits of his co-religionists, who have often been fuzzy on issues of membership. (John said the real issue was not membership; it was baptism.) John was no doubt talking more about deliberation than about worship when he said no one should be excluded. **"I don't like abuse in the name of God,"** he said.

--No idea is too crazy to be listened to. (I was often, in an interpersonal way, the beneficiary of John's practice of that virtue.) **"To be disarmed after the mode of Christ is to be endowed with the power of truth telling...and community building, for which the metaphors of cosmic conflict are most apt because they break the frame of normalcy."** John Yoder listened for metaphors of cosmic conflict. He listened everywhere to Calvinists, Jews, Catholics, Lutherans--and even, to my dismay, anthropologists such as René Girard.

--Communal moral reasoning begins at both ends. That was an important corrective in my formulation of the Yoderian things I was trying to say to other lawyers. It is not (as we, trained as we were in the manipulative processes of appellate legal literatures, think) so much a matter of formulating one of our legal issues and then "taking it to the church"--although it could be that. It is as well a matter of beginning in the church: **It is possible, John said, to begin with gospel notions "and then work out from there...rather than beginning with the 'real world' out there and then trying to place the call of God within it." The discerning community as epistemology.**

* * *

And so, John, my friend, good-bye. I will talk to you later.

www.ingramcontent.com/pod-product-compliance
Lightning Source LLC
Chambersburg PA
CBHW071451160426